MEDIA ANALYSIS - THEORY

Flash cards, graphic organisers, templates, drop-down lists, summaries and subject-specific vocabulary to assist with study, essays and Media terminology.

Year 11 and 12 Media Production and Analysis

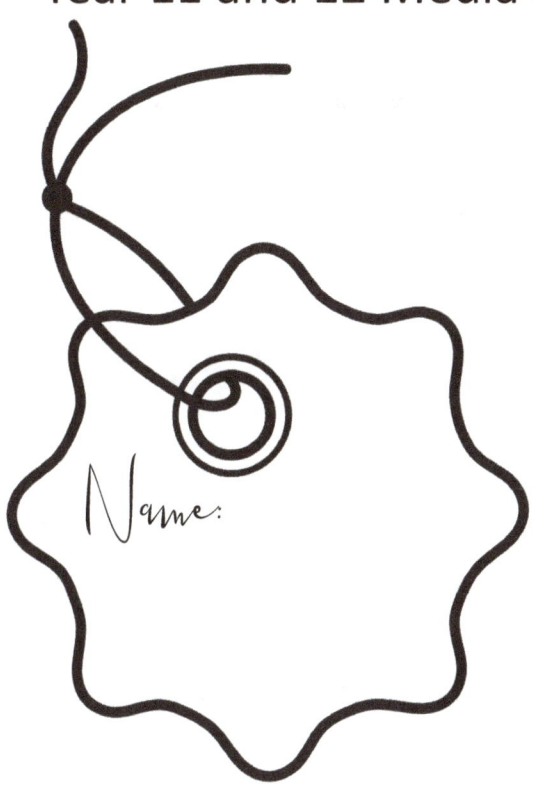

COPYRIGHT
© Lisa Merante 2023
All rights reserved.

No part of this publication may be reproduced, stored in a retrieval system, or transmitted in any form or by any means, electronic, mechanical, photocopying, recording or other means, now known or hereafter invented without the prior permission of the author and publisher.

Trademark notice: the use of product or corporate names has been done so for identification purposes only, with no intent to infringe.

Every effort has been made to acknowledge and attribute authorship of copyrighted material. Should any errors have occurred the publisher would welcome information to assist in ensuring accuracy with information in any future editions.

Photocopying beyond that set out by fair dealing requires written permission from the publisher.

Publisher: Media and English Literacy Publishing
For secondary senior school age.
Mass Media—textbooks.

Disclaimer:
QR Codes and URLs were accurate at the time of publishing. Neither the author nor publisher is responsible for URLS changing or expiring.

ISBN: 978-0-6453498-2-5 (paperback)

First Edition 2023

Lisa Merante is a Media teacher with more than 30 years of experience in her field. Her commitment to Media Studies has seen her involved in exam writing for Australian Teachers of Media Western Australia (ATOMWA) and exam marking for School Curriculum and Standards Authority (SCSA). She has had three students achieve the Subject Exhibition Award in Media Production and Analysis. Lisa has taught internationally and is currently working at an independent public school in Western Australia.

Thank you
ACKNOWLEDGEMENTS

I would like to thank:

- My family - to my husband Darryn, my son Callum, and mother Elizabeth, thank you for making my life richer.
- Bec Hamblin - for your friendship and counsel.
- My students - who put up with my repeated use of the words 'specificity' and 'drop-down list' without too much groaning.
- Last, but not least, my teaching colleagues, particularly Chris Gooch and Callum Hunter whose feedback and encouragement throughout the writing process have been hugely appreciated.

Table of CONTENTS

Chapter One — 8
Plan to succeed
- Plan to succeed 9
- Goal setting 11
- Due dates 12
- Revision timetable 13
- Assessment Tracker 14
- Topics to revise 16

Chapter Two — 18
Codes and conventions summary
- Media codes 19
- Symbolic code 20
- Written code 21
- Audio code 22
- Technical code 23
- Conventions 26

Chapter Three — 28
Flash cards
- Flash Cards 29
- How to use the flash cards ... 30
- Year 11 flash cards 32
- Year 12 flash cards 44
- Drop-down list flash cards ... 60

Chapter Four — 72
Terminology
- Media terminology 73
- Terminology 74
- Command verbs 81
- General sentence stems 84
- Transition words 85
- Ways to describe camera movements ... 86
- Ways to describe camera shots ... 87
- Ways to describe sound 88
- Ways to describe editing 89

Chapter Five — 92
Essay structure
- Essay structure 93
- Essay formula 94
- Essay plan 95
- T.E.E.L structure 99
- Signal verbs 100
- Formatting quotes 101
- Structure strips 104

Chapter Six — 106
Graphic organisers
- Graphic organisers 107
- Study flash cards 108
- Study flash card template 109

- Study graphic organiser template 110
- Graphic organisers 140
- Codes graphic organiser template 142
- Target audience graphic organiser template 143
- Narrative elements graphic organiser template .. 144
- Context graphic organiser template 145
- Values and ideologies graphic organiser 146
- Representations graphic organiser 147

Chapter Seven — 148

Drop-down list of essential content

- Essential Content drop-down list 149
- Year 11 drop-down lists of essential content 150
- Year 12 drop-down lists of essential content 160
- Sample drop-down list............. 170

Chapter Eight — 172

Media theories summary

- Summary of media theories 173
- Summary of communication theories 174
- Summary of narrative theories............ 176
- Summary of representation theory 180
- Summary of auteur theory 182
- Summary of genre theory................ 184
- Summary of identity theory................ 185

Chapter Nine — 186

Practice, organise, de-stress

- Organise your thoughts 187
- Notes, notes, notes............. 188
- Media Terminology 236
- Film & TV recommendations 266
- Podcast recommendations 267
- Website recommendations............. 268
- Book recommendations............. 269
- Colour-in, de-stress, relax 271
- Interesting Ted talks............. 274
- Index 276
- Bibliography............. 277

Film Trivia
Useless Facts

- The producers of the movie *Gone With The Wind* were fined $5,000 for allowing the word "damn" to be heard within the movie's dialogue.

- Alfred Hitchcock used chocolate syrup to portray the blood in the shower scene in his classic film *Psycho*.

- The first toilet to be flushed in a motion picture was in Alfred Hitchcock's movie *Psycho*.

Chapter One
Plan to succeed

- Goal setting
- Assessment due dates
- Revision timetable
- Assessment tracker
- Topics to revise

Study habits

Plan to succeed

Motivation

Goal setting is the way to build a path to success. Everyone's view of success is different. Do not compare your wants and desires with someone else's. Stay true to you. Set your own goals. Why is this important at the start of a Media Compendium I hear you ask? Because, if you want to achieve well in anything you need to plan for it to happen, you need to take steps to make your concept of 'success' happen. In this chapter you will find templates to assist you with goal setting. Be organised, work out when assessments are due, when you can allocate time to work on revision, and when you need to work on production and theory assessments.

If you fail to plan, you plan to fail.

- **Set your goals.** Work out what you would like to achieve by the end of the course.
- **Write the goals down.** Make them tangible, manageable, and achievable.
- **Set deadlines.** If you have time limits, you are more likely to actively work towards achieving specific aspects of your goals.
- **Reflect on your goals.** Be accountable for what you set out to do. If circumstances change, be flexible and adjust accordingly.
- **Persevere.** Having the resilience to try and try again will ensure that you move forward.

A goal without a plan is just a wish.

Antoine de Saint-Exupéry

Course GOAL SETTING

What course grade would you like to achieve?

State the study habits needed to achieve your goal.

01

02

03

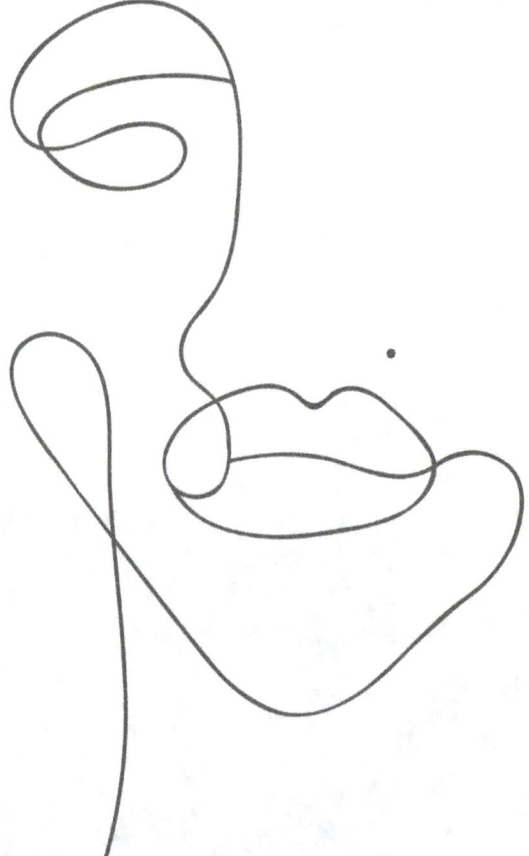

Atomic Habits by James Clear is a useful and accessible book on creating habits that better position you to achieve your goals. It has been on the New York Times best seller list, and is a highly recommended, worthwhile read.

"The best way to predict the future is to create it."

—Erich Fromm

Goal setting

Check-in

Check in every term to re-evaluate your goals. What have you done well? What could you do better? What steps are you going to put in place to ensure you can successfully achieve your goals?

☐	Term 1
☐	
☐	
☐	
☐	
☐	
☐	
☐	
☐	
☐	

☐	Term 2
☐	
☐	
☐	
☐	
☐	
☐	
☐	
☐	
☐	

☐	Term 3
☐	
☐	
☐	
☐	
☐	
☐	
☐	
☐	
☐	
☐	

☐	Term 4
☐	
☐	
☐	
☐	
☐	
☐	
☐	
☐	
☐	
☐	

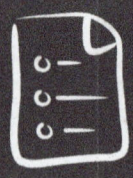 **Due dates** — *Assessment*

January	February	March
April	May	June
July	August	September
October	November	December

Revision timetable

Revision

	ESSENTIAL CONTENT TO REVISE	CHECK
MON		☐ ☐ ☐ ☐
TUE		☐ ☐ ☐ ☐
WED		☐ ☐ ☐ ☐
THU		☐ ☐ ☐ ☐
FRI		☐ ☐ ☐ ☐
SAT		☐ ☐ ☐ ☐
SUN		☐ ☐ ☐ ☐

Assessment Tracker

ASSESSMENT	GRADE	
	WEIGHTING	%
1.		
2.		
3.		
4.		
5.		
6.		
7.		
8.		

FEEDBACK	IMPROVEMENT GOALS

Topics to revise

Revision

NOTES

YEARS 11 & 12

- ☐ Representations and stereotypes
- ☐ Values and ideologies
- ☐ Audience (mainstream and niche)
- ☐ Subculture, social groups
- ☐ Context
- ☐ Theme
- ☐ Narrative elements
- ☐ Narrative structure
- ☐ Theme
- ☐ Controls and constraints
- ☐ Point of view
- ☐ Trends
- ☐ Communication theories
- ☐ Narrative theories
- ☐ Codes
- ☐ Conventions
- ☐ Commercial and independent media
- ☐ Globalisation
- ☐ Documentary techniques
- ☐ Selection, emphasis, and omission
- ☐ Encoding, decoding
- ☐ Preferred, negotiated, oppositional meaning

ADDITIONAL CONTENT

- ☐ Stuart Hall - Representation theory
- ☐ Stuart Hall - Reception Theory
- ☐ Claude Levi-Strauss binary oppositions
- ☐ Todorov's narrative theory
- ☐ Stephen Neale - Genre theory
- ☐ Communication theories
- ☐ Narrative theories
- ☐ Conglomerates
- ☐
- ☐
- ☐
- ☐

Topics TO REVISE

NOTES

YEAR 11

- ☐ Popular culture
- ☐ Realism
- ☐ Classification and censorship
- ☐ Journalistic media
- ☐ Concentrated media ownership issues
- ☐ Audience reach
- ☐ Immediacy, accessibility
- ☐ Influential media
- ☐ Ethical and legal issues and consequences

YEAR 12

- ☐ Aesthetics
- ☐ Auteur
- ☐ Film movements, media in different times
- ☐ Niche audience
- ☐ Marketing, production, distribution, and exhibition
- ☐ Persuasive techniques
- ☐ Propaganda
- ☐ Censorship
- ☐ Dangers in naturalising stereotypes

Chapter Two

Codes and conventions summary

- S.W.A.T defined
- Symbolic codes
- Written codes
- Audio Codes
- Technical Codes
- Conventions

Flash cards for concept learning

Media codes

S.W.A.T codes

Choice of symbolic + written + audio + technical codes = constructed preferred meaning

Media productions are constructions, they are built using a **choice of codes**. The codes are often chosen or manipulated to suit audience expectations of genre. The audience has a historical understanding of how **codes** are combined to form meaning in narratives. **Codes and conventions** work hand-in-hand. As a **convention** is the expected practice or established way of using **codes** they can be utilised to either subvert, challenge, or reinforce viewer expectations.

To make a media production, numerous codes must be selected, when combined they form a preferred meaning for the audience.

SYMBOLIC

- Objects
- Colour
- Setting
- Body language
- Costume
- Hair & makeup
- Facial expressions
- Mise-en-scène

WRITTEN

- Captions
- Headlines
- Titles
- Speech bubbles
- Typography choice
- Credits

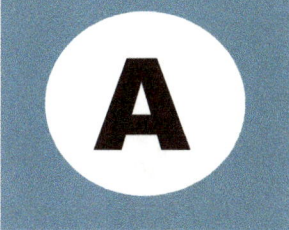

AUDIO

- Music
- Dialogue
- Sound effects
- Voice over
- Atmosphere
- Rhythm, volume, pace, and pitch
- Silence

TECHNICAL

- Shot sizes
- Camera angles
- Camera movements
- Lighting, exposure
- Shutter speed
- Compositional techniques
- Lens choice
- Editing choices - graphic, spatial, temporal, or rhythmic
- Special effects

Symbolic code

| OBJECTS | COLOUR | COSTUME | SETTING |

BODY LANGUAGE

HAIR & MAKEUP

FACIAL EXPRESSIONS

- → **Objects** assist in creating the world of the narrative, or they may be used as plot progression points, such as using a map to find a lost item.

- → All **colours** have connotations derived from their context. e.g., a red rose connotes love.

- → **Costume** includes clothing, hair, make-up, and facial expressions which assist in constructing characters and era.

- → **Body language** is central to developing mood and assisting with character creation.

- → **Setting** creates a sense of time and place.

- → **Mise-en-scène** refers to all the elements included in a scene to create realism, including symbolic and audio codes.

Written code

Codes

TITLES	CAPTIONS	HEADLINES	CREDITS

SPEECH BUBBLES

TYPOGRAPHY

- Written codes assist in anchoring meaning to an image.

- Headlines assist to narrow the interpretation of an image or body of work. They appear in large type at the top of an image or section of text and are often written by the copy editor to suit the target audience of a publication.

- Captions appear beneath an image and assist to clarify meaning.

- A title sequence presents the leading cast, crew, and title of the production. The closing credits acknowledge the work contributions of all cast and crew.

- Typography choice reflects the style and genre of the production.

- Speech bubbles are predominantly used in comics to convey the narrative by providing dialogue or insight into a character's thoughts and conversations.

Audio code

Diegetic sound originates from a source within the world of the film and can be heard by the characters. e.g., dialogue between characters, sounds made by nature, a dog barking and music which originates from the story world such as a character listening to a radio are all diegetic as they belong to the world of the narrative. Diegetic sound is crucial for creating realism for the audience which assists them to suspend their disbelief and engage with the fictional world.

Non-diegetic sound originates from outside of the film world. These sounds cannot be heard by the characters and include the music score or a voice over. Non diegetic sound is external to the world of the narrative, there is no visible source for the sound to be emitting from within the fictional world.

| MUSIC | DIALOGUE | SOUND EFFECTS | SILENCE |

- **Music** is used to indicate moments of heightened emotional intensity or to signify light relief and is used to set the overall mood, and tone for the story.

- **Dialogue** is used to convey the plot and to define characters through what they say and how they say it.

- **Sound effects** such as footsteps, clothing movement, stirring a coffee or creaking floorboards are added to match the image and enhance the realism of the fictional world.

- **Voice-over** is non-diegetic and allows the audience to see the narrative unfold from the point of view of the narrator.

- **Atmosphere** or **ambient** sound: every location has a particular sound; to create realism this sound needs to be captured or manufactured to allow for expected location sounds such as birds chirping, cars passing, wind blowing, children playing, and so on, to be heard in the scene.

- **Rhythm, volume, pace, and pitch**: the flow, tempo, tone, and volume are elements of sound, that can be used to emphasise information about characters, action and genre.

- **Silence** is the absence of any sound. When used effectively it can create emotional intensity, tension, and unease.

Technical code

| LIGHTING | CAMERA MOVEMENT | CAMERA ANGLE | SHOT SIZE |

→ **Lighting** is used to create a specific atmosphere. Dark lighting creates an ominous feel, whereas bright lighting tends to feel more cheerful.

→ **Shot sizes** function to convey information. For instance, a close-up reveals detail such as emotion and an extreme long shot highlights the setting or action.

→ **Camera movements** include, but are not limited to, tracking, panning, zooming, tilting, and dollying.

→ **Camera angles** include, but are not limited to, high camera angle which suggests the subject is small and vulnerable, low camera angle which suggests the subject is large and dominant, an eye-level camera angle which creates a feeling of equality, and an aerial view which establishes geographic location.

→ **Compositional devices** include leading lines, rule of thirds, juxtaposition, contrast, and positioning.

→ **Editing choices** set the style, pace, and rhythm of the narrative by manipulating time and space through editing techniques such as graphic match, transitions, match on action, cross-cutting, cutaways, jump cuts and the use of montage.

→ **Lens choice,** including shutter speed and aperture direct viewer attention.

→ **Special effects** include physical visual effects for character construction, green screen to create the realistic illusion of places or things and computer generated effects to create the world of the film.

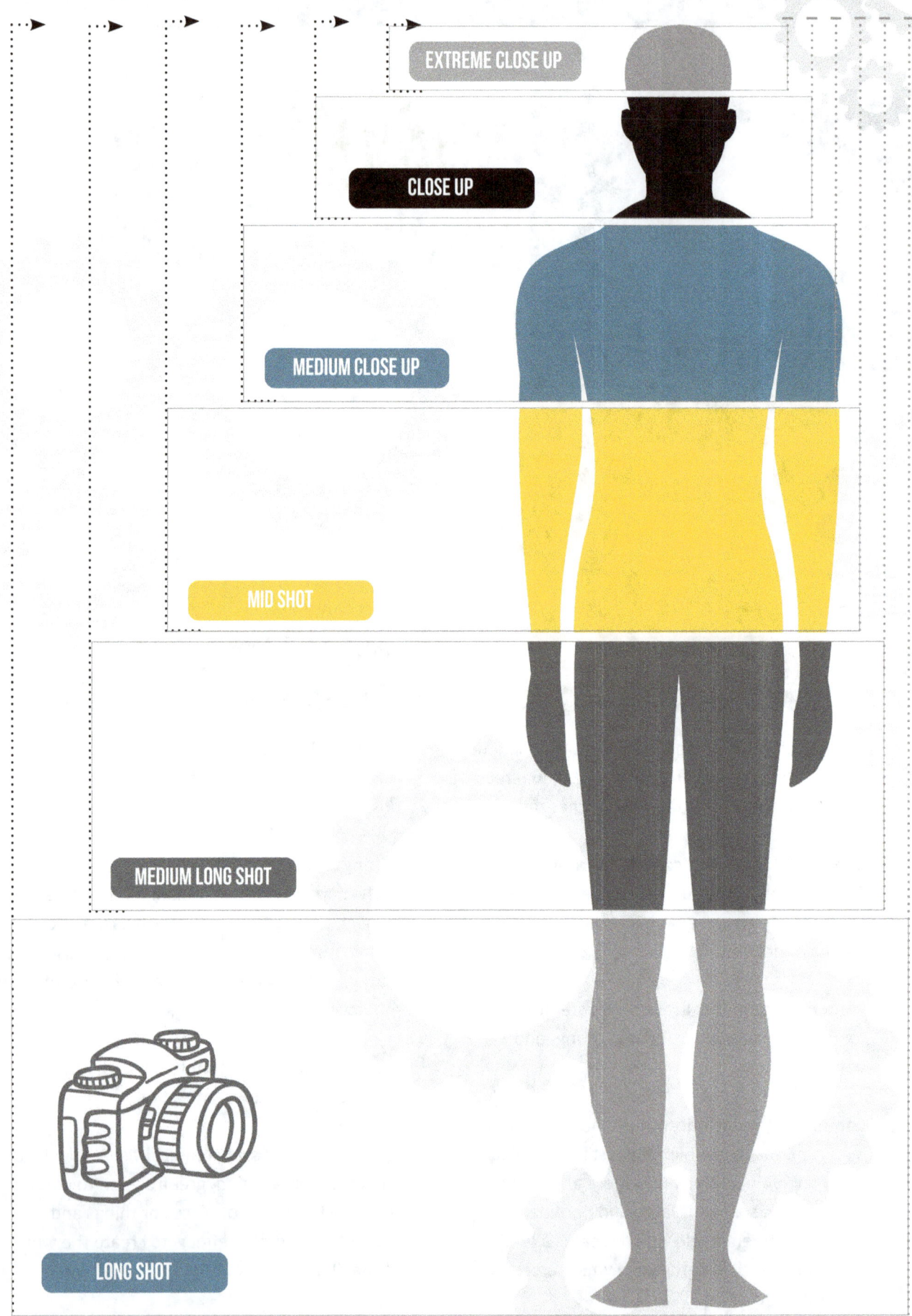

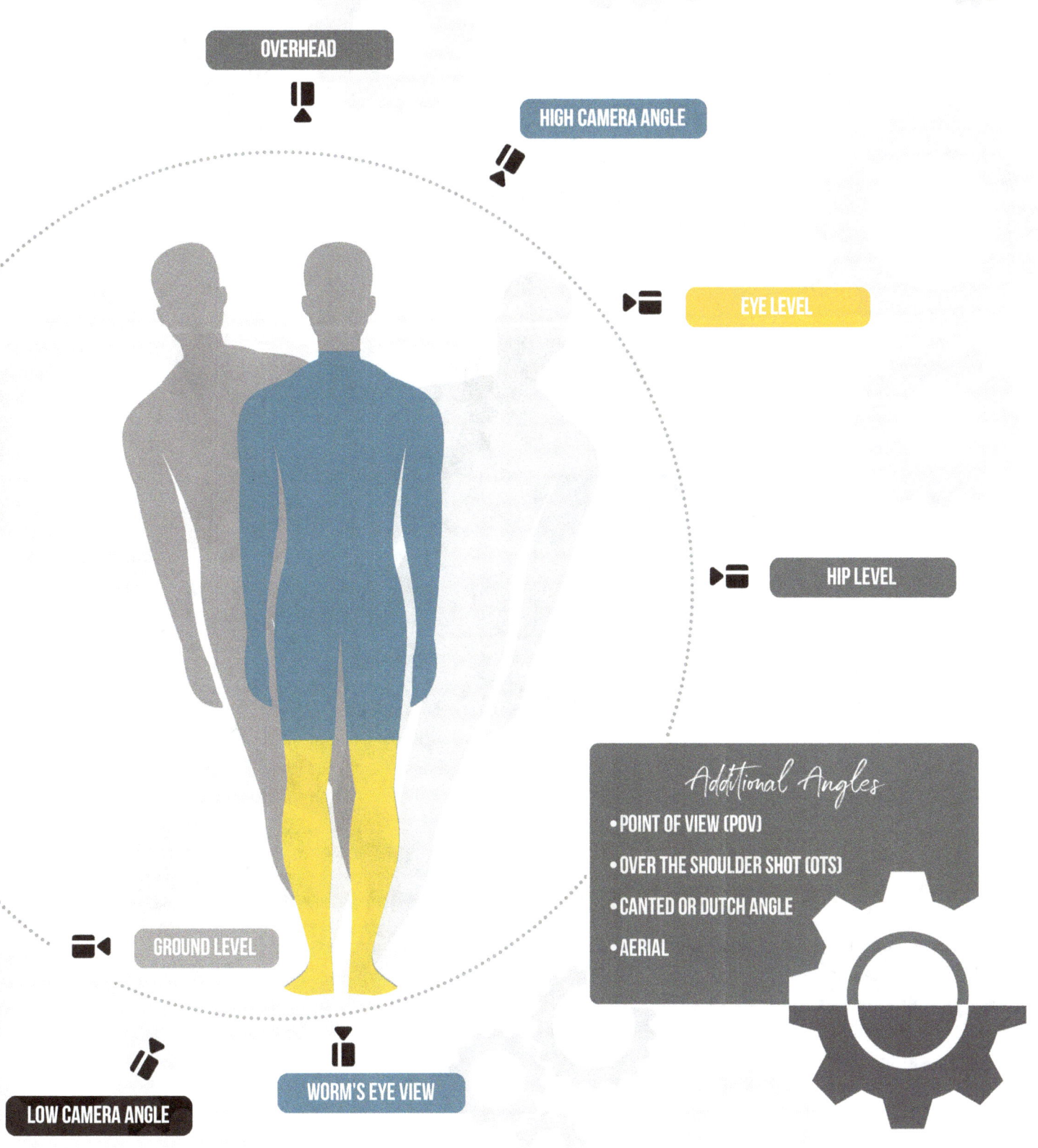

Conventions

Conventions are the expected practices or established ways of using **codes and techniques** to construct meaning. They can be used to either subvert, challenge, or reinforce viewer expectations and include expected ways of structuring a narrative, using iconic elements of a genre, manipulating time and space and conventional expectations of form.

Conventions such as:

- audience expectations of mise-en-scène
- manipulation of time and space
- narrative construction
- editing
- conventional use of codes and film grammar

Narrative conventions such as:

- creation of point of view to foreground the protagonist
- use of narrative elements
- conventional use of narrative structure such as linear cause and effect.

Genre conventions such as:

- iconography associated with specific genres. e.g., cowboys, deserts, saloons, guns used in western genres.
- conventional audio codes associated with specific genres e.g., suspense music used in thrillers.
- conventional settings, characters, style, and narrative structure.

Conventions

 *Expected Practices*

Documentary conventions such as:

- interviews, testimonials
- archival and black and white footage
- re-enactments
- emotional appeal
- voice over, narration
- authority figure
- statistics
- emotive appeal
- selection and omission
- bandwagon, straw man, oversimplification, card stacking, common man, stereotyping ...

Film movement conventions such as:

- French New Wave: use of jump cuts, long takes dominate, breaking of the fourth wall, open-ended resolution ...
- Film Noir: conventionally uses chiaroscuro lighting, includes a femme fatale, first person voice over narration ...
- Hollywood: linear cause and effect plot construction leading to a clear resolution, goal orientated characters, seamless and invisible use of film making processes ...
- Surrealism: anti-narrative, desire to shock, non-linear, fractures time and space ...
- German Expressionism: exaggerated sets used as an extension of character psychology, chiaroscuro lighting, canted angles, dark themes ...

Editing conventions such as:

- eye-line match, including the 180° rule used to position the characters and create a consistency in screen space.
- manipulation of time e.g., flash forward, flashback, slow motion, split screen ...
- manipulation of space. e.g., a siren indicating extended space beyond the frame, or a character exits the frame and the audience actively fills in the details as to where they have gone.
- rhythm and pace (created through sound, cinematography, and editing)
- editing - used to establish screen space and narrative time, leading the viewer to understand what is important within the narrative. Conventions include:
  → montage refers to the ordering of shots in a sequence which facilitates the manipulation of time and space thus suggesting a world beyond the boundary of the screen frame
  → continuity editing: seamless, invisible, screen direction flows, eye-line match is used to position the characters and create a consistency in screen space, all allowing for suspension of disbelief.

Television conventions such as:

- segmentation
- repetition
- immediacy
- novelty
- planned flow

Flash cards

- How to use the flash cards
- Year 11 flash cards
- Year 12 flash cards
- Concept drop-down list flash cards

Flash cards for concept learning

Flash Cards

How to use

➡ Do you know your media terminology? Marks are attributed to you being able to seamlessly incorporate media terminology and concepts into your writing. The flash cards can be used to test your knowledge on major concepts. Practicing with frequency as part of your study program will embed the terminology into your working memory.

➡ It is important to be able to use the specialist terminology of any subject you are studying. By doing so you are demonstrating mastery and a command over your subject matter. You will be able to communicate your knowledge effectively to assessors by consistently using relevant subject specific terminology thus improving your grade.

➡ **Directions for use:**
1. Photocopy the pages and cut up the sections applicable to your year group into flash cards.
2. Test your knowledge by placing the essential content terms down on a flat surface and then attempt to match the term to its correct definition.
Or
3. Photocopy and turn into traditional flashcards with the essential content term on one side and the definition on the other. Practice recall by yourself or with others.

- → Use the flash cards to assist you with definitions.
- → Practice incorporating the terms into your answers.
- → Review the terminology on a regular basis to move terms from your short term memory into your long term memory. Looking at the flashcards the night before an assessment will have limited impact; incorporate them into a study routine.
- → As part of your study regime, practice active recall, have someone test you by using the flashcards to see what you remember. With regular practice you will be able to incorporate the subject terminology in a more consistent and relevant manner into your answers.

How to use the flash cards

The flash cards are designed to teach concepts and to create a scaffold for answering potential exam questions.

THIS PART IS IMPORTANT

1. **DO NOT** try and regurgitate definitions in an exam unless the question asks you to do so. The examiner knows what these terms mean. They are looking to see how you apply the concepts to a text, NOT how you define a term.
2. **DO NOT** try and apply every single aspect of a concept to a question. For example you may get an exam question which looks something like this:

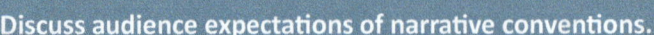

> Discuss audience expectations of narrative conventions.

There are two parts to this question (a) audience expectations and, (b) narrative conventions.

You have a lot of **possible content** to choose from to answer this question, but you must narrow it down. Let's list the **possible content:**

(a) Audience expectations - have they been met, challenged or subverted?
  - define who the primary and secondary are for the text
  - state the audience expectation of content based on the marketing of the text and its genre
  - expectation of narrative structure
  - expectation of narrative elements
  - expectation based on point of view

(b) Narrative conventions
  - narrative structure (linear cause and effect, elliptical etc.)
  - narrative theory (Todorov, Levi-Strauss)
  - genre conventions (structure, iconography)
  - narrative elements (character, setting, conflict, resolution)
  - point of view (from whose eyes does the narrative unfold?)
  - manipulation of time and space (flashback, flash forward, open frame ...)
  - narrative sequence (how does the opening establish character intentions, themes, and possible progression points?)

How to use the flash cards

 For you to show depth of knowledge you need to have ONE main point per paragraph and explain it in depth with relevant textual examples to justify your claims. Clearly, the list of possible content to answer the question is WAY too much to fit into a timed essay. You need to make an educated choice as to what elements best answer the question and suit your chosen text.

 So, what should you do? Why study all the content if you are not actually going to apply it? Well, different questions require different elements in the answer. We never know what the examiners will throw at us, so it is better to have a lot of content in our tool bag and pare it back, rather than not enough.

 One possible way to narrow down the essential content would be to start with the first two dot points under audience expectations and then discuss narrative structural conventions in relation to expectations of genre conventions and apply narrative theory. To do this in detail under timed exam conditions would take the allocated time. You could touch on narrative elements such as expectations associated with characters who are villainous and those that are heroic and link them to audience expectation of narrative, particularly genre. However, as time in an exam is limited, you should focus on writing in detail on the above mentioned aspects of narrative conventions, clearly link them with audience expectations and leave the other content points alone. It is better to show depth of knowledge, supported by clear textual evidence rather than try to cover every possible aspect of narrative, which does show breadth, but not depth.

 Point being:
By learning the essential content terms and concepts associated with the course you will be able to draw on an entire tool bag full of knowledge which you can then confidently apply to your class texts.

Confidence comes from being prepared

-John Wooden

Year 11 flash cards

In Year 11 you are expected to build a strong foundation of knowledge, particularly by accurately using the course terminology with consistency and relevance. By creating a rich Media vocabulary, you will be able to draw on a pool of knowledge when tackling assessments. Understanding key terms clarifies your comprehension of the essential content.

... are the building blocks used to construct meaning in media texts. They include the symbolic, written, audio and technical codes which are chosen to construct a preferred meaning.

- ... are the expected practices or established ways of using codes. They can be used to either subvert, challenge, or reinforce viewer expectations.
- Conventions include, but are not limited to, expected ways of structuring a narrative, utilising iconic elements of a genre, manipulating time and space and conventional expectations of form.

- Costume
- Setting
- Objects
- Body language, including facial expressions, hair, and make-up
- Colour
- These codes create meaning beyond the literal.

- Music
- Dialogue, including accent and vocabulary choice
- Sound effects
- Voice over narration
- Use of silence
- Consideration of rhythm, volume, pace, and pitch

- Titles
- Credits
- Captions
- Speech bubbles
- Headlines
- Typography choice

- Camera angles, movement
- Shot sizes, framing
- Lighting, shutter speed, aperture
- Lens choice
- Leading lines, rule of thirds, juxtaposition, contrast, positioning
- Special effects
- Editing choices - graphic, spatial, temporal, or rhythmic

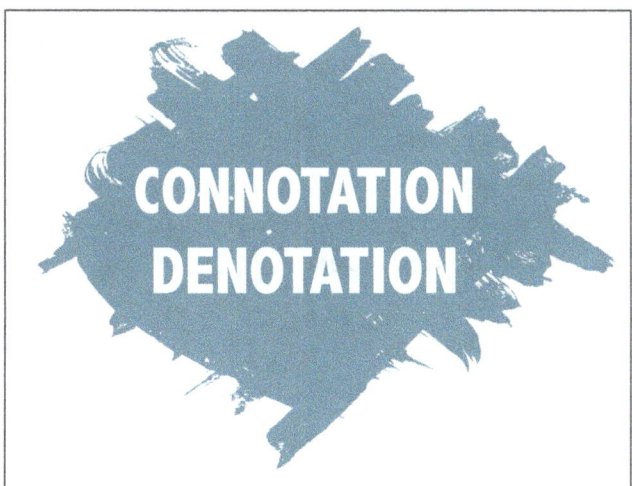

- All codes have a denotative meaning and a connotative meaning. In other words, the code has a literal meaning and a deeper or associated meaning. e.g., red rose - denotative meaning is a flower, connotative meaning suggests love.

- The values, traditions, norms, and artefacts embraced by the majority of people in a society which deliver a distinctive zeitgeist or personality to an era. The cultural climate is circulated via institutions, media, family, and friends.

- Is the beliefs, practices and products embraced by the masses.
- Elements which signal popular culture are mass popularity, ease of accessibility, mass production and commercialisation, items or ideas offer instant gratification and their constantly evolving nature reflects their cultural context.
- Iconography (common icons which indicate an era).

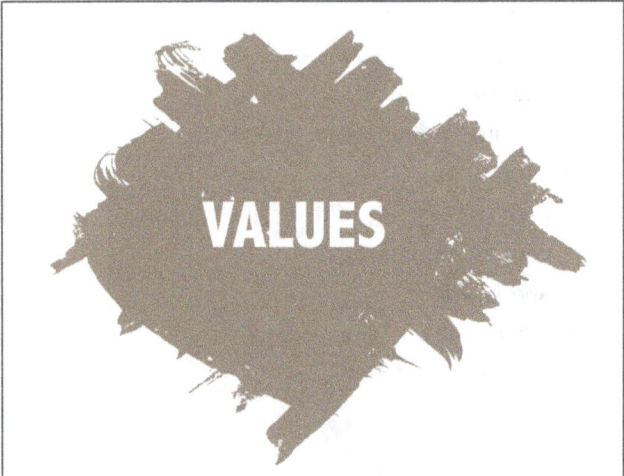

- Refers to what members of a culture deem worthy, aspirational, or desirable. Positive values act as a guide for appropriate behaviour.
- What values are revealed by a character's actions and appearance?
- What values and ideologies are revealed in the conflict and resolution?
- Values and ideologies are contextual. What do they say about the culture of the time?
- Consider ethics, ideals and conduct.

- Refers to a shared collection of values, attitudes and beliefs that structure and shape a society.
- Texts can support, challenge, or subvert ideologies.
- The media plays a role in disseminating ideologies. Common ideologies are:
  ○ familial
  ○ patriarchal
  ○ capitalism
  ○ environmentalism

- → Attitudes are how a person feels, thinks, and behaves towards other people, events, objects, ideas, and situations.

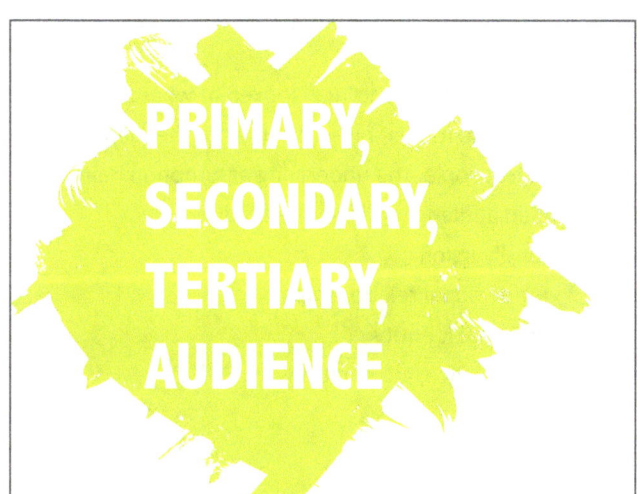

- → The **primary audience** is the main **target audience**. The content and message of the text is designed to engage with them by connecting with their **demographic, geographic and psychographic metrics.**
- → The main content is not directly targeted or intended for the **secondary audience**, however they will frequently engage with it due to their connection with the primary group.
- → The **tertiary audience** are people on the periphery; they are outside of the direct intended circle of recipients for the content.

- → The public can be made up of small **niche** groups or larger **mainstream** groups who consume media content through the lens of their **demographic, psychographic** and **geographic** factors.

- → Reception Theory
- → Uses and Gratifications Theory
- → Hypodermic Needle Theory
- → Reinforcement Theory
- → Agenda Setting Theory
- → Spiral of Silence
- → Diffusion of Innovation
- → Semiotic Theory
- → Two Step Flow Theory
- → Cultivation Theory

Stuart Hall states we have a 'shared cultural map' which places a framework around how an **active audience decodes** a text.

1. Dominant or preferred reading – the audience shares and accepts the intended meaning.

2. Negotiated reading – the audience understands the dominant position but doesn't necessarily subscribe to that ideology.

3. Oppositional reading – whilst understanding the dominant meaning, the audience chooses to reject it.

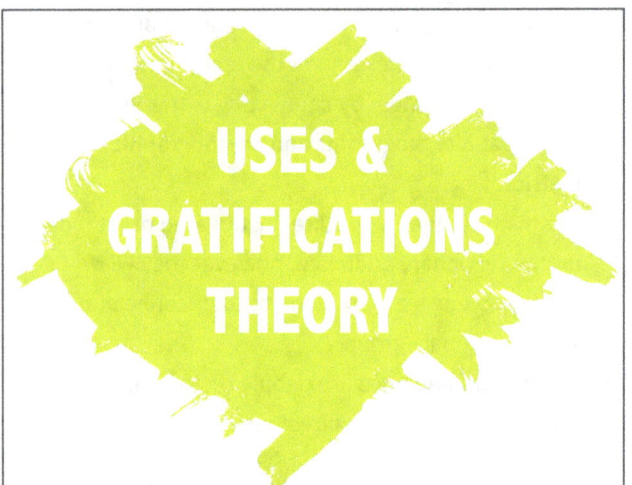

Blumler, Katz and McQuail looked at what people do with the media, rather than what the media does to people, the underlying assumption being that an audience will use the media:
- for diversion
- for personal relationships
- personal identity
- surveillance, information.

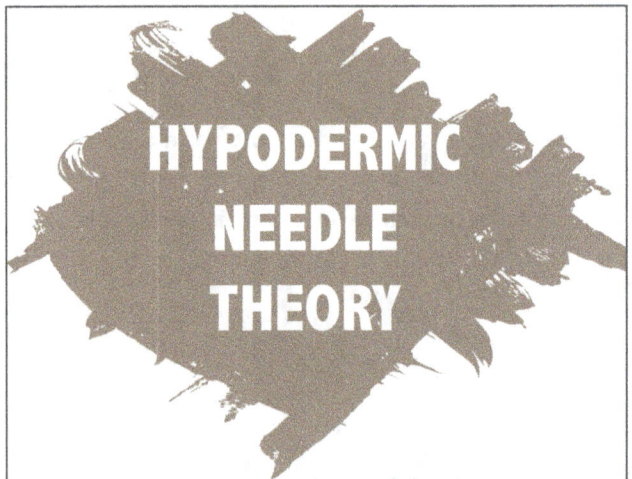

Sometimes called the **Magic Bullet Theory or Direct Effects Model** because it felt the media was so powerful it could 'shoot' messages straight into the audience's mind. The theory suggests that media content is injected directly into an audience's consciousness without the individual filtering or mediating the message in any way.

The outdated theory suggests that the audience is passive, homogeneous, and easily susceptible to media manipulation.

McCombs and Shaw posited that the media can't tell the audience what to think, but they can tell them what to think about. Characteristics include:
- Framing (selection, emphasis, exclusion, elaboration)
- Priming
- Gatekeeping

Elisabeth Noelle-Neumann (1974) examined why people stay silent on issues of importance when they judge that their view differs from the majority. This retreat into silence occurs from a fear of social isolation, a fear that if they speak up, they will be ostracised.

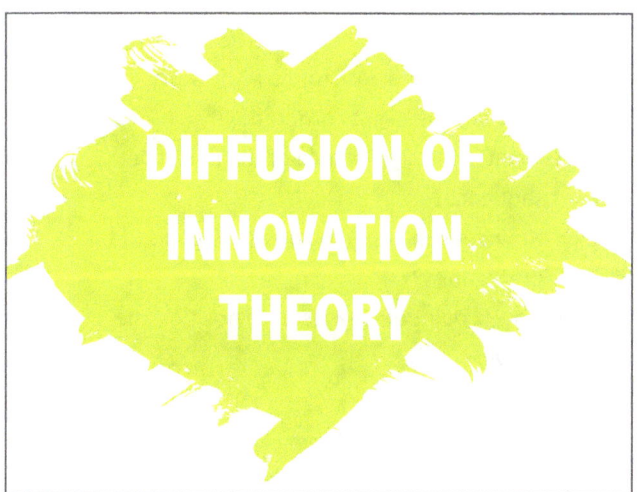

Everett Rogers, (1962) examined how and why an innovation (new idea, product, behaviour, technique, belief, process, service, or new technology) spread over time and space in a predictable manner. He categorised people into five groups:
- innovators
- early adopters
- early majority
- late majority
- laggards

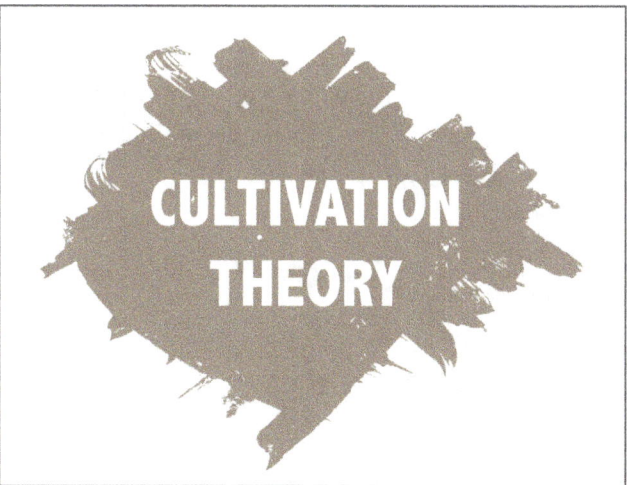

- Conceptualised by George Gerbner and Larry Gross the theory looked at the effect of habitual, **cumulative exposure** of television and how this impacted people's beliefs and vision of their social reality.
- Heavy viewers of television **cultivated** what Gerbner, and his colleagues coined the **'mean world syndrome'** whereby people who continuously viewed violent TV shows saw their real world as dangerous and were less trusting of other people.

Joseph Klapper (1960) promoted the idea that audiences would be more likely to accept and support an idea if it already aligned with their pre-existing values and ideas. The audience actively uses media by:
- selective exposure
- selective retention
- selective perception

The basic elements contained in narratives are:
- characters
- setting
- conflict
- resolution

These elements are the scaffold upon which the story and plot are built.

... is the framework for how the story unfolds.
- How are the events ordered?
- What is the significance of the narrative sequence?
- How does the opening posit the goals of the protagonist?
- How is point of view used to position the viewer?

Todorov's structuralist approach to narrative theory posits that stories follow a similar pattern consisting of five distinct stages. These being:
- equilibrium
- disruption
- recognition
- repair
- reinstatement

...is a strategy used to construct the narrative. Through which character(s) perspective is the audience positioned to view the action? All media texts, whether fiction or non-fiction, construct a specific point of view. Codes and conventions position the audience to support the preferred meaning by aligning them with the values embedded in the protagonist's actions, appearance, and behaviour.

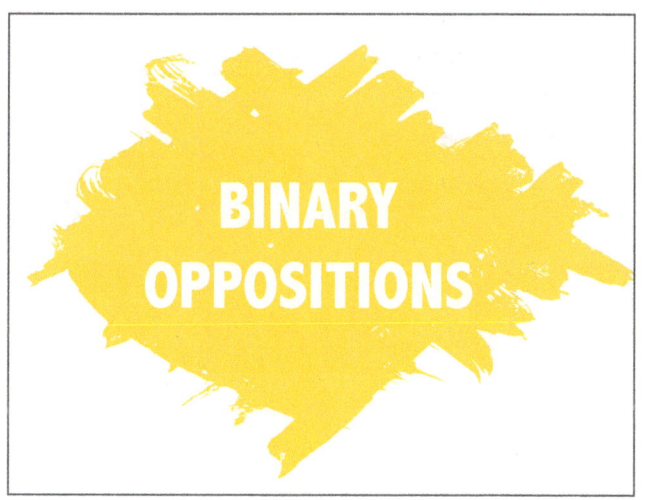

- Claude Lévi-Strauss suggested the idea that binary oppositions are used in narratives to fuel audience engagement by creating contrasting characters and ideas.
- Fundamentally, for conflict to exist in a narrative, binary opposites must be present. This creates an opposition between the forces of good and evil or hero and villain.

- Television narrative includes characteristics such as immediacy, narrative complexity, segmentation, repetition, novelty, flow, and open-endedness. Narrative construction is impacted by ratings and scheduling.

Gustav Freytag diagrammed a method of mapping a story's progression in the shape of a pyramid which follows the course of a five act play. The five elements being:
- exposition
- rising action
- climax
- falling action
- denouement

- … create a framework for scaffolding the narrative progression of the plot. e.g., Gustav Freytag's pyramid, Claude Lévi-Strauss' binary oppositions, Tzvetan Todorov's theory of equilibrium, disequilibrium, and enigma.

- The audience has an expectation of the plot structure and events depending on the genre.
- Stephen Neale's theory of repetition and difference posits that the audience requires repetition for familiarity, however difference is required to maintain continued interest in the genre.
- Iconography is what we visually associate with a genre. e.g., in a western, cowboy hats, sheriff and jails are some iconic elements that shape the genre.

- ... is the main message which recurs throughout the narrative. A theme is also known as the moral, main idea or unifying concept within the story.

- Narrative montage: the cutting and ordering of shots to manipulate time and space.
- Ideational montage: images linked or juxtaposed together to create an idea.

Refers to the background behind a fact, event, period, or the circumstances surrounding an event. Context ALWAYS affects content.
Consider the impact of:
- cultural context
- historical context
- social context
- political context
- economic context

How we communicate verbally, through written language and body language on any given topic or issue creates a discourse, or a way of thinking about the subject matter. A dominant discourse surrounds all issues as the way people behave, act, write or talk about an issue reflects the dominant values and ideologies in society.

→ ... exists within the main culture. Groups of people with similar interests, beliefs, and values form subcultures. Subcultures assist with identity formation as people can signal their belonging to a group.

→ ... are recurring representations which are constructed from easily identifiable general traits, which, when used repeatedly, can become naturalised.
→ Stereotypes form around repeated use of generalised physical traits or behaviours which create a short cut in meaning for an entire group.

- Representations in media texts re-present a filtered version of reality to the audience; it is not the real world but a mediated version of the world.
- Mediation occurs through:
    → Codes of construction
    → Values embedded in the choice of codes
    → Context: how does the representation reflect or challenge cultural and social norms?
- Representations have the power to control the construction and circulation of meaning.

How have the following influenced the decoding of a text?
- → choice of codes and conventions to encode meaning.
- → choice of representations to circulate meaning.
- → selection and omission - what ideological viewpoint is privileged?
- → can you apply a communication theory to examine how, or if, mass media influences the audience?

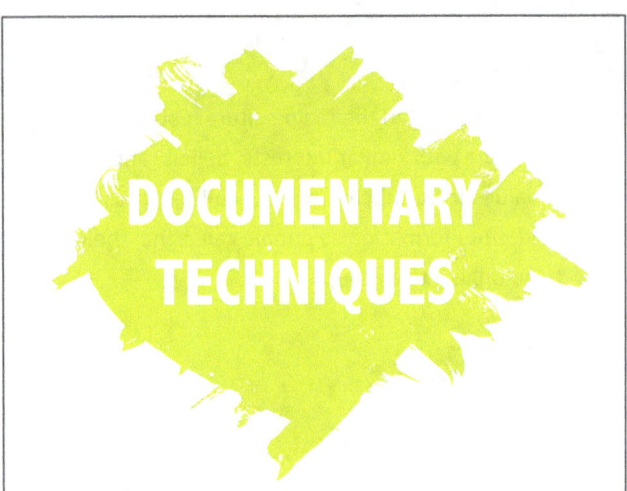

- → Voice over narration
- → Testimonial
- → Interview
- → Black & white footage
- → Re-enactments, dramatisation
- → Archival footage
- → Juxtaposition
- → Exposition
- → Authority figures
- → Emphasis, assertion
- → Statistics
- → Actuality footage
- → Selection & omission
- → Emotive appeal
- → Bandwagon
- → Card stacking
- → Glittering generalities
- → Name calling
- → Oversimplification
- → Common man
- → Scapegoating
- → Agenda setting
- → Stereotyping/labelling

- → A media monopoly has the potential to influence the nation's ideological agenda.
- → Better to legislate for media diversity to allow for competing voices to be heard.
- → Cross-media ownership allows for a powerful presence in the media landscape.
- → Media ownership matters as it can narrow the range of content available to an audience and reduce accountability.

- → Moral, ethical, and legal - such as regulatory bodies and codes of practice.
- → Technology - access and innovation are competing issues.
- → Production constraints - time, budget, personnel, resources.
- → Censorship and classification - ACMA regulates Australian media by specifying rules for all content, including advertising.
- → Audience expectations regarding values, structure, genre, codes, and conventions ...
- → Institution and ownership - what is the agenda?

Realism in fictional texts revolves around media productions constructing a mediated sense of reality. The media text represents a version of reality to its audience constructed from a choice of codes and conventions

Literally means to put in place. This includes all elements within the film's frame which assist the audience to suspend their disbelief and engage with the world of the narrative. Discuss elements such as motifs, costumes, objects, audio, choice of actors, lighting …

- → A new direction media is headed in terms of style, content, technologies …
- → A shift in representations, particularly of minority groups and women.
- → Shift from linear to non-linear content.
- → The rise of misinformation, disinformation, and fake news.
- → The creation of information echo chambers and filter bubbles.
- → Simultaneous, multi-platform consumption of content.

The time period in which a production is made is different to when it is set. How do values, ideologies, technology, and so on, present at the time of production, influence its content?

Year 12 flash cards

In Year 12 you are expected to use the terms learnt in the Year 11 course and build on them. The flash cards on the following pages pertain to the Year 12 course. Keep using the Year 11 flash cards but now add in the Year 12 concepts and terminology to enhance your grade.

PROBLEMS WITH STEREOTYPING

- Simplification arises due to the narrow choice of codes used as a short cut in meaning to construct a representation, thus leading to inaccuracy.
- Selection and omission – what is excluded what is foregrounded? Representations privilege certain views, ages, ethnicities, genders and so on. Whose agenda is served?
- Bias - consider social, political, emotional, financial, or physical repercussions.

AUTEUR

… is someone whose films show a signature style, technically and thematically across a body of work. An auteur can be a director, screenwriter, producer, cinematographer, editor, music composer, costume designer, actor, production designer, or even a studio - the defining characteristic is that their filmography shows a clear and recognisable stylistic or thematic signature.

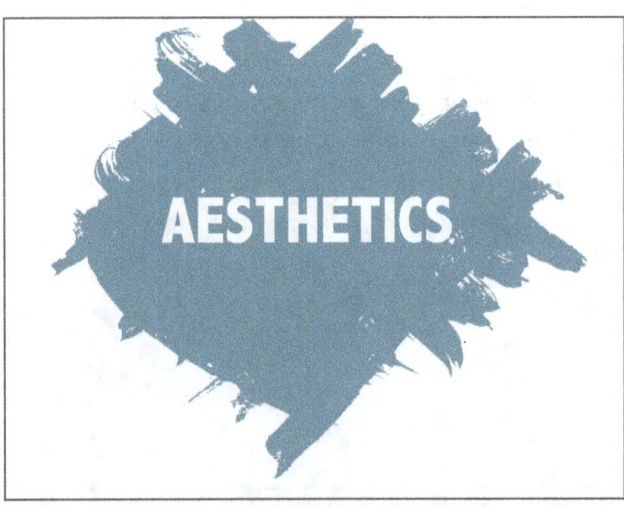

AESTHETICS

… is concerned with the style and form of film, it is about the film maker's intention, and the viewer's reception, in terms of appreciating the creative, symbolic, and expressive intent. Often these defining factors can be seen as a deviation from, or a rejection of, the mainstream Hollywood formulaic narrative.

- is the intention to make a social or political comment or to explore an issue?
- loose association given to cause and effect, and narrative closure is not emphasised.
- less emphasis is placed on action and more on the emotional driver of the protagonist.
- experiments with codes and conventions to manipulate, innovate and extend the boundaries of accepted film grammar.
- art films direct their content to a small, niche audience of like-minded people.
- often use lesser known or amateur actors.

... act as a time capsule by reflecting the cultural, economic, political, and social elements of the society from which they arose. They highlight what is relevant and authentic to filmmakers and audiences during that moment in time. E.g., French New Wave, German Expressionism, Film Noir, Surrealism ...

- innovative visual aesthetic
- manipulation of narrative structure
- character subjectivity
- open-ended narrative
- political and social comment
- manipulation of time and space
- deviation from realism
- experimentation with rhythm, pace, and continuity editing
- manipulation of the medium

- is someone who is well-established and well-known in their field.
- he or she is awarded for achieving excellence in their domain.
- an iconic figure can be an auteur, actor, camera person, editor, script writer or anybody who is iconic within their area of work.

- Alternative film refers to movies whose content and style provide an alternative to mainstream Hollywood formulaic commercial narratives.
- Experimental: the filmmaker experiments with the medium, technology, style, and structure of the media work.
- Most alternative and experimental films fall into the independent film category.

An independent film is any movie made outside of the major Hollywood style systems which embraces innovation in terms of aesthetics, style, codes and conventions, narrative manipulation, technology ...
- small budget with the majority of funding being derived from outside of major studios.
- emphasis on character development and emotional impact.
- original narrative in terms of theme, may comment on social issues, particularly those that the mainstream media shy away from.

- A question on artistic style is asking you to draw on your knowledge of auteur theory, aesthetics, film movements, codes and conventions of art films and narrative structure.

Personal expression is linked to auteur theory but not necessarily across a body of work. Possible discussion points:
- aesthetics
- manipulation or use of art film codes and conventions
- experimentation or manipulation of narrative
- context - expression regarding issues, beliefs and so on.

- A distinctive aural aesthetic constructed from recurring motifs such as music, sound effects, or a particular recurring piece of dialogue which signals a change of direction in the narrative.
- Any recurring sound which is used to create an emotional and intellectual response to the narrative.

- A distinctive visual aesthetic is constructed from the use of numerous recurring motifs such as objects, colour palette, camera movements, editing techniques, costumes and so on to clearly convey the theme of the media text.

Editing - used to establish screen space and narrative time, leading the viewer to understand what is important within the narrative. Conventions include, but are not limited to:
- the use of montage
- continuity editing
- eye-line match
- manipulation of time and space
- use of rhythm and pace.

- Social or political trends e.g., trend of environmental awareness.
- Consider films which actively challenge the established trends of cinema through manipulating aspects such as narrative structure, characterisation, and visual aesthetic.
- Trends in the way audiences engage with and interpret media work (think communication theory).
- How changing technology trends affect media use e.g., trends in genres, music, special effects ...
- Trends in the perception and representation of gender, race, and sexuality.

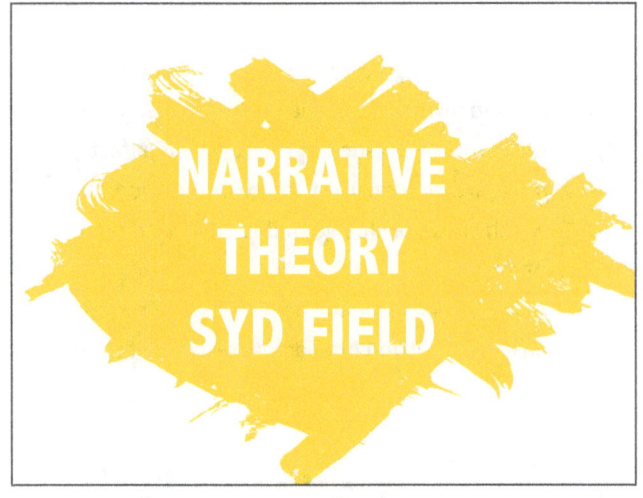

→ Syd Field proposed the three act structure consisting of the set-up, confrontation, and resolution. His theory is visually represented as a triangle with the climactic moment being at the top.

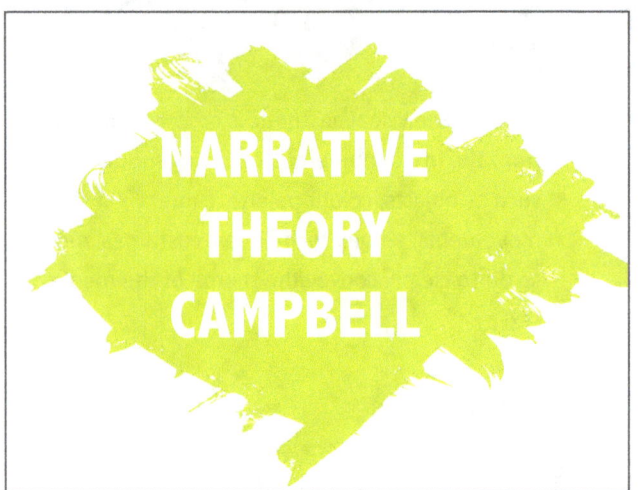

→ Joseph Campbell's 1949 plot template refers to the structure of stories which follow the narrative progression of an unwitting hero who finds himself on a journey, learns something about himself, at a decisive moment in the plot puts this new-found knowledge to use, triumphs over adversity, then returns home transformed by his adventure.
→ N.B. The use of pronouns reflects the era.

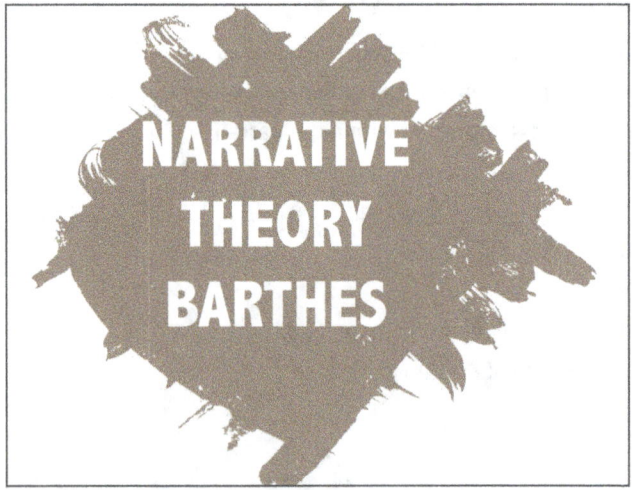

Roland Barthes suggested that stories contain five main narrative codes which the audience can use to decode the plot.
→ Enigma code
→ Action code
→ Semantic code
→ Symbolic code
→ Referential code

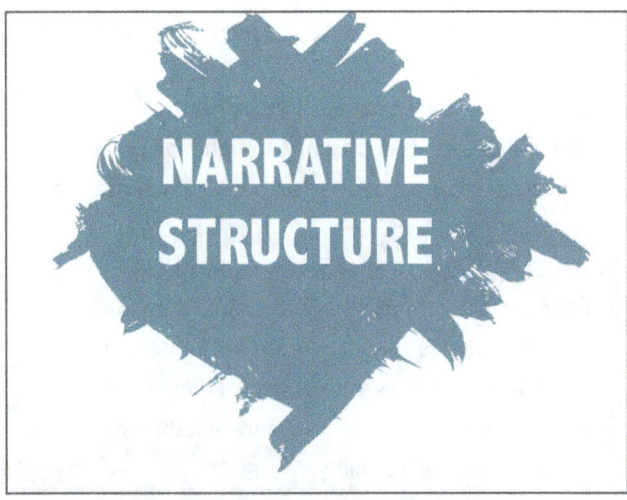

Narrative structure refers to the framework for how the story events are ordered.
→ Multi-layered includes multiple plot lines
→ Linear cause and effect create a chronological sequence to the narrative.
→ Non-linear narrative is disjointed or fractured.
→ Circular narrative begins and ends at the same point.
→ Multi-layered includes multiple plot lines.
→ Episodic is told in flashbacks, flash forward or chapters.

Vladimir Propp identified eight character roles that he attributed narrative functions to:
- hero
- villain
- dispatcher
- donor
- princess
- helper
- false hero
- father

Possible content to discuss:
- Narrative structure - does the text use a conventional linear cause and effect structure or does it subvert conventional structures?
- Can you apply narrative theories? Does the text follow a conventional story structure pattern?
- Are conventional genre expectations met or subverted?
- Are conventional narrative elements used to meet audience expectations or challenge them?

Possible content to discuss:
- Does the text use a conventional narrative structure, or does it manipulate conventional structure?
- Discuss the manipulation of time and space.
- Discuss the manipulation of narrative elements.
- Discuss the manipulation of genre conventions.
- Discuss manipulation of conventional story structures.

- Focused, small, targeted segment of the audience.
- Smaller, but still influential group with specific interests.
- Niche productions are financially riskier due to their smaller audience base.
- Link the media content to the beliefs and values of the niche audience.

- Real time vs. screen time.
- Compressed time - graphic match, transitions, fast motion, simultaneous time, jump cuts ...
- Expanded time - freeze frame, slow motion, replay, cutaways, repetition ...
- Time manipulation techniques - flash back, flash forward, dream sequence, long take ...
- Temporal order, duration, and frequency.
- Linear and non-linear delivery

- Sound from a source outside of the frame suggests the surrounding space and atmosphere.
- Film space is primarily manipulated through sound, montage, and mise-en-scène.
- Mise-en-scène assists the audience to suspend their disbelief and engage with the fictional film space. The director, working with the set designer will use spatial elements such as props, setting, costume, colour, and acting performance to create the fictional film space.

- Means 'cinema truth', an observational cinema style which attempts to document realism. It conveys a sense of authenticity by being a 'fly-on-the-wall', observing and documenting what unfolds rather than constructing a narrative. The dialogue, actions, setting and so on are not scripted but arise naturally out of the situation.

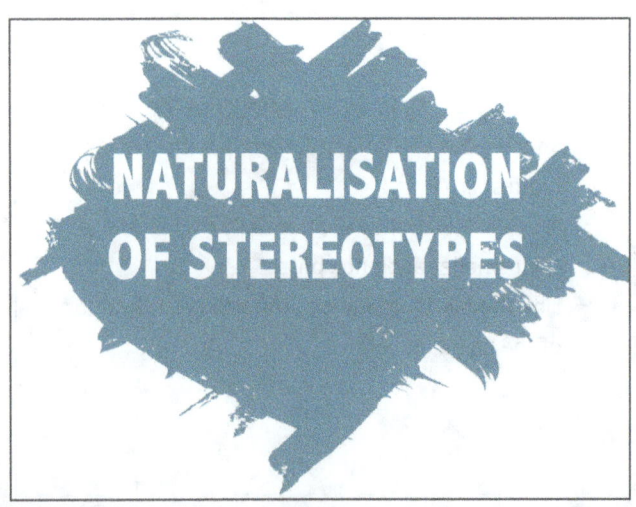

- The codes used to form stereotypes are repeated with frequency, making them the natural and accepted way to view the group. The naturalisation process makes it difficult, but not impossible to shift attitudes regarding the group.
- Oversimplification leads to inaccuracy. The process of choosing and repeating a few codes to represent the entire group means that generalisation and simplification occurs, narrowing the frame of reference regarding the group.

- The world of the narrative.
- An audience will suspend their disbelief and engage in the diegesis of the film.

Hegemony is the process of a group in society having power over others, not through coercion but with consent, with the subordinate group believing it is in their best interests to accept and adopt the dominant ideologies. For example, capitalism: we know it ultimately benefits a few, however we believe that capitalism will allow equal access to all.

- Refers to the removal of media content deemed offence, inappropriate or a threat. Carried out by government boards such as the Australian Classification Board.
- Self-regulation: e.g., Hays Code, codes of conduct
- Ratings system: places films into categories for various audience demographics depending on the suitability of content in relation to violence, sexuality, coarse language ...

- To propagate or spread ideas or information in a deliberate manner designed to influence other's beliefs, attitudes and behaviours about a cause, institution, or person.

David Gauntlett, a British media theorist and sociologist specialises in the relationship between digital media and audiences. Gauntlett discusses the symbiotic relationship between consuming and creating in a digital landscape. He expresses how modern audiences, in their ability to produce their own media content, influence the construction of how their identity is represented.

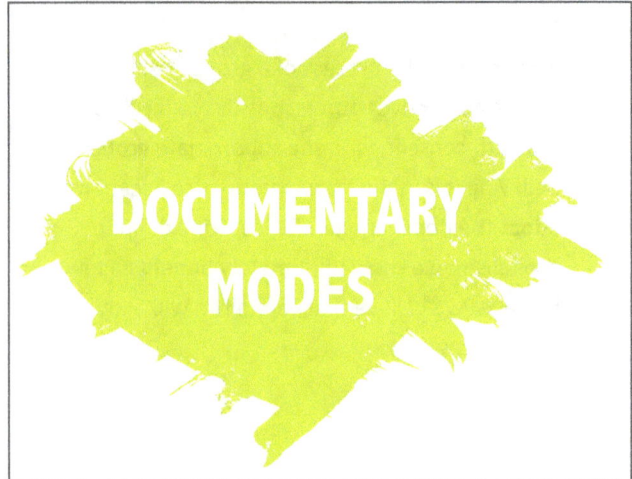

Documentary modes such as those posited by Bill Nichols:
- expository
- poetic
- reflexive
- observational
- participatory
- performative

- Selection: prioritising certain issues over others
- Emphasis: highlighting an issue, possibly through repetition. e.g., how many days does an item stay in the news cycle?
- Exclusion: omitting items from the agenda.

These terms, commonly associated with the Agenda Setting Theory can be applied to news, documentaries, and fictional narratives.

- How does funding impact the content of media productions? Does the funding source impact the agenda?
- Allows for diversity of views only if alternate non-commercial media is funded.
- Government funded media, is it partisan or bipartisan?
- Impacts technology, cast, crew, marketing, distribution.
- Can foster innovation.

- Refers to world-wide shared values, ideologies and beliefs disseminated via mass media. Often linked with cultural imperialism as the source of information can saturate smaller entities with its own culture. Consider how American films, music and television shows pervade the world.

Possible content:
- Function of commercial vs non-commercial media
- Mainstream vs niche audience
- Agenda of institution
- Technology enabling prosumers
- Funding
- Audience expectation

Consider any technique which has the power to persuade an audience:
- choice of codes such as colour palette, music, lighting, camera movement, shot composition ...
- conventions associated with form such as documentary conventions, news conventions ...
- editing: e.g., juxtaposition, montage
- narrative sequence and narrative structure
- emotional appeal techniques
- Choice of symbolic, written, audio and technical codes.

- Refers to the power to make decisions regarding journalistic content such as text, images, sound, editing, publication, distribution, funding, staffing. Who has the power to construct the narrative and set the agenda?

- → Framing refers to what news information is selected and what is omitted to 'frame' or compose news items.
- → Priming refers to the time, space and coverage provided to an issue, making some issues prominent and ignoring, or giving minimal coverage, to others.
- → Gatekeeping refers to people, such as a news editor, who decide (through selection and omission) the content of media publications.

→ Regulation examples: Australian Broadcasting Corporation Act 1983 ensures independent delivery of high quality Australian fiction and non-fiction content. ACCC - Australian Competition & Consumer Commission regulates Australian media …
→ Codes of Practice examples: Commercial Television Industry Code of Practice, the Commercial Radio Code of Practice, the Australian Press Council …
→ Censorship is linked to power and agenda-setting.
→ Ethics addresses moral issues in relation to media content, access to media, ownership, distribution …

- → Discuss how a fiction or non-fiction text comments on a social or political issue reflective of its context.
- → Power of media content to influence an audience's beliefs, values, and ideologies.
- → Codes, conventions, and techniques used to construct political or social comment.
- → Bias inherent in construction (selection, omission).

- → Ethical
- → Legal, including copyright
- → Funding
- → Conflicts of interest
- → Context issues. e.g., representation, or issues surrounding Covid (who can film, where and so on).

- A level playing field occurs when people can access media despite socio-economic, geographic, and demographic barriers. For instance, accessing content on free-to-air or Netflix.
- Global access means that producers need to adjust content to consider, not just the domestic market, but an international viewing audience as well.
- Global access links to casting and representation of characters as there is the need to identify in a culturally sensitive manner for a wider audience.

Possible theories to consider:
1. Communication theories such as Reception Theory, Uses and Gratifications Theory, Reinforcement Theory, Agenda Setting Theory, Spiral of Silence, Diffusion of Innovation, Semiotic Theory ...
2. Narrative theories such as Claude Lévi-Strauss' binary oppositions, Tzvetan Todorov's theory of equilibrium, disequilibrium, and enigma, Propp's theory of character functions, Joseph Campbell's Hero's Journey, Barthes' narrative codes, Syd Field's 3 Act Structure.
3. Stephen Neale's Genre theory.
4. Stuart Hall's Representation theory.

- Stuart Hall posits that we have a "shared cultural map".
- For the map to make sense we classify and name things using language (spoken, aural, visual, written or any sign system). Language choice is shaped by context.
- Representations take shape through language. Hall states that without language (sign systems) meaning could not be exchanged.
- Representations are not neutral, they are shaped by context and reflect the agenda of those with power.

- Contextual information informs meaning by providing a back-story regarding the narrative's cultural context which may consider historical context, political context, economic context and social context.
- Context always affects the content of a narrative.
- The cultural context of an audience can impact the interpretation of a text.

Stuart Hall's Reception Theory posits that the producer encodes meaning into a media text considering the choice of codes, conventions, audience expectations and controls and constraints. The audience decodes the media text considering their interpretation of the choice of codes, their understanding of conventions and their dominant values, beliefs & ideologies to arrive at a:
→ dominant or preferred reading
→ negotiated reading or
→ oppositional reading of the text.

How do the chosen conventions privilege the filmmaker's point of view? Consider the use of:
- → voice over
- → testimonials and interviews
- → archival footage
- → re-enactments, dramatisations
- → juxtaposition
- → exposition
- → authority figures
- → statistics
- → selection, omission, emphasis

→ Where, when, and by whom a media product is made, shapes its content. Includes:
- ○ Context - historical events, values and attitudes present in a particular era, popular culture trends which impact on content of media work ...
- ○ Controls and constraints - legal and ethical considerations, classification boards and regulatory bodies, codes of conduct ...
- ○ Technological and production factors - time, budget, cast and crew, audience expectation of genre or auteur ...
- ○ Institutional factors - agenda, intended audience ...

→ Links to genre as the marketing content is shaped by genre expectations
→ Audience expectation of media content based on marketing.
→ Cross-platform promotion to target intended audience demographic.

- What codes and conventions have been selected to construct the narrative?
- What values are embedded in the selection of specific codes?
- What has been omitted? Why?
- What is the intended impact of selection and omission?

- Commercial media: content is aimed at a large mainstream audience. The focus is on ratings and profit. Funded by advertisers or subscriptions.
- Non-commercial media: provides a public broadcast service. Funded by the government.

How does the agenda drive the filmmaker's point of view?
- What is the filmmaker's agenda?
- How is the film being funded? Does the institution or source of the money come with an agenda attached?
- Consider shareholders and their influence.

- Consider how large corporations like Walt Disney Company own numerous media assets and therefore have a global presence which can shape audience perception through their huge distribution of content.

→ Who is the intended audience? How does the marketing campaign target them? How has audience expectations of genre been used to publicise the film?

→ Distribution and publicity are linked. They describe how a film is delivered to an audience. What are the avenues for distribution? How does the audience know the film exists? Consider the importance of film trailers, advertising, interviews, film premières, film critic reviews and so on to connect with the intended audience.

→ Exhibition - where and when is the film screened? Is it in a mainstream cinema, independent cinema, or released straight to a streaming source?

Drop-down list flash cards

How to use

Using the drop down list

- The flash cards are designed to summarise main areas of learning and to give you an easily retrievable list of points to discuss in relation to the concept in an exam or in-class assessment situation. If you use the 'drop-down' list method of knowing what a term means, and what points to discuss in relation to that term, you will be able to scaffold your answers against the 'drop-down' list points.
- This system saves you time as you are not staring into space wondering what to discuss when faced with the essential content point in a timed assessment. If you know your drop-down list in relation to the major concepts you will be well placed to succeed.
- Remember that you need to supply at least one, but preferably more specific textual examples to evidence every single one of the concepts you discuss from the drop-down list.
- The flash cards on the following pages list the content associated with an essential term. The lists are mostly hierarchical and designed to help you scaffold you answer by following the points in sequence.

REPRESENTATION

Re-present a filtered version of reality to the audience; it is not the real world but a mediated version of the world.

1. State the **representation.**
2. Discuss the **choice of codes** used to construct the representation.
3. Discuss the **values** embedded in the choice of codes.
4. Discuss **contextual** factors which shaped the representation. How does the representation reflect or challenge cultural and social norms?
5. Representations have the power to control the construction and circulation of meaning.

NARRATIVE

Is the linking of cause and effect to tell a story which arises out of a specific context.

1. **Narrative elements** (character, setting, conflict, resolution).
2. **Narrative structure** is the framework for how the events unfold. e.g., linear cause and effect, elliptical, episodic. How does the opening position the audience? How are events ordered?
3. **Narrative theory** e.g., Claude Lévi-Strauss' binary oppositions, Tzvetan Todorov's theory of equilibrium, disequilibrium, and enigma.

SUBCULTURE

A group existing within the main culture with different beliefs.

1. State the subculture and explain how it deviates from mainstream culture.
2. Discuss how people **signal their belonging to the group** by discussing aspects such as **clothing, speech patterns, behaviours, activities, and actions.**
3. Discuss their **values and beliefs** - what do they value? How does this deviate from the norm? Subcultures often resist or deviate from aspects of the dominant culture.

POINT OF VIEW

Point of view is a strategy used to construct the narrative. Through which character(s) perspective is the audience positioned to view the action? Codes and conventions position the audience to support the preferred meaning by aligning them with the values embedded in the protagonist's actions, appearance, and behaviour.

1. Specify from **whose eyes** does the narrative unfold from.
2. Discuss the **codes** used to construct a specific point of view which position an audience to support an idea, issue or character in a positive or negative way.
3. Discuss the **values** embedded in the character's point of view. How is the audience asked to view the issue/topic/person etc?
4. How does the point of view assist in constructing the **preferred meaning** of the text?

SYMBOLIC CODES

Setting, colour, body language, clothing and objects.

1. State the **symbolic codes** used to encode meaning.
2. Discuss the **connotations** of the codes and how they position the audience to deconstruct the text.
3. Discuss the **values embedded** in the choice of codes.

AESTHETICS

Is the study of what makes a film artistic, what makes it visually and aurally appealing.

- mise-en-scene, colour palette, visual and aural motifs, technical codes ...
- manipulation of narrative structure, open-ended narrative
- character subjectivity
- political and social comment
- manipulation of time and space
- deviation from realism
- experimentation with rhythm, pace, and continuity editing
- manipulation of the medium

AUDIENCE

Complex groups of people with histories, experiences, and values which they bring to their consumption of media texts.

1. State the intended audience. Explain the primary audience in terms of their demographic, psychographic and geographic metrics.
2. Discuss audience expectations (of genre, of narrative, of characters ...)
3. Consider audience/communication theories e.g., Reception Theory, Uses and Gratifications, Agenda setting ...
4. Audience values - relate to preferred meaning.

MEDIA THEORY

Refers to any model or study which examines the impact media content has on a mass audience or explains a concept, supported with evidence relating to mass media.

Chose a theory. Discuss the relevant points.
- **Narrative theories** create a framework for scaffolding the narrative progression of the plot. E.g., Freytag's pyramid, Todorov's theory.
- **Communication theorists** have investigated how audiences interpret and use the media they consume. E.g., Reception Theory ...
- Stephen Neale's **Genre theory**
- Stuart Hall's **Representation theory**
- Andrew Sarris' **Auteur theory**
- David Gauntlett's **Identity theory**

THEME

The main message which recurs throughout the narrative. A theme is also known as the moral, main idea or unifying concept within the story. Theme is communicated to the audience via visual and aural devices.

1. State the theme/s.
2. What codes and conventions have been employed to construct **characters** and in doing so represent theme? Deconstruct the actions, behaviours, values, dialogue, and intentions of the main characters
- How do the chosen **codes and conventions** communicate the theme. What **values and ideologies** are embedded in the theme?
- Does the **setting** allow for the characters to reveal or reinforce the theme? How does the **conflict** and **resolution** convey the theme?

INDEPENDENT FILM

Film makers working outside of large institutions such as a large studio system.

1. State the independent film company
2. Discuss the film maker's intent - usually an original or controversial story or theme.
3. Specify the funding source. Discuss the use of the small budget to innovate and experiment ...
4. Discuss emphasis on character development and emotional impact.
5. Consider experimentation with conventional rules of film grammar.

NICHE AUDIENCE

A focused, small, targeted segment of the audience. A smaller, but still influential group with specific interests. Niche productions are financially riskier due to their smaller audience base.

1. State who the niche audience is. Be specific, use demographic metrics.
2. Discuss how niche audiences tend to have specific interests and engage with content which deviates from the mainstream. How is the content different - consider themes, aesthetics, narrative structure ...
3. Discuss the values, beliefs, interests and so on of the niche audience.

HALL'S RECEPTION THEORY

How an audience is positioned to view a text: dominant, negotiated, or oppositional reading. Stuart Hall states we have a 'shared cultural map' which places a framework around how an active audience decodes a text.

- A text is constructed using a choice of codes and conventions. The audience is positioned to decode meaning in three main ways:
1. Preferred reading - the audience shares and accepts the intended meaning.
2. Negotiated reading - understands the preferred reading but doesn't necessarily subscribe to the ideology.
3. Oppositional reading - understands the dominant reading but rejects it.

VALUES

Something people believe in or aspire to. Values refers to what members of a culture deem worthy, aspirational, or desirable. Positive values act as a guide for appropriate behaviour.

1. State the main values.
2. Does the text promote, **challenge, reinforce, endorse** or **subvert** the dominant values?
3. What values are suggested by the **actions, appearance** and **dialogue** of the protagonist and antagonist?
4. What values are embedded in the **conflict, and resolution**? What is suggested to be worth fighting or striving for?
5. Values and ideologies are contextual. What do they say about the culture of the time?

IDEOLOGIES

Refer to a set of beliefs or practices that enable a society to function in an organised way.

1. State the main ideologies.
2. Which ideologies are **privileged** in the text? Which are **challenged**?
3. Discuss ideologies embedded in characters, conflict, and resolution.
4. What **message** is encoded in the foregrounding of certain ideologies?
5. Does the texts can support, challenge, or subvert ideologies?

ENCODING/DECODING

Meaning is created through the choice of specific codes, conventions, and techniques. The audience unpacks the meaning based on their demographic metrics.

1. State the codes and conventions used to encode meaning.
2. Encoding considerations: audience expectations, values and ideologies of the era, constraints ...
3. Discuss how an audience is positioned to decode meaning. Reference Stuart Hall. Consider how an audience interprets the choice of codes according to their dominant values and beliefs.

TECHNICAL CODES

Shot sizes, camera angles, camera movement, lighting, composition, editing.

- Technical codes are:
    - shot size, framing
    - camera angle, movement
    - lighting
    - compositional devices such as leading lines, rule of thirds, juxtaposition, contrast, positioning
    - editing choices

PERSUASIVE TECHNIQUES

Any technique which has the power to persuade an audience to respond to a particular argument, character, or point of view

---

State choice of codes such as colour palette, music, lighting, camera movement, shot composition ...
- → conventions associated with form such as documentary conventions, news conventions
- → editing - e.g., juxtaposition, pace, rhythm
- → narrative elements and narrative structure
- → emotional appeal techniques
- → Choice of symbolic, written, audio and technical codes

CONTEXT

Refers to the background behind a fact, event, period, or the circumstances surrounding an event. Context ALWAYS affects content.

---

1. State the context
- → Contextual information informs meaning by providing a back-story regarding the narrative's cultural context which may consider historical context, political context, economic context, cultural context, and social context.
- → Context always affects the content of a narrative.

MONTAGE

Meaning is created by editing shots together in a particular sequence to manipulate time and space.

---

1. Discuss how time and space is manipulated
- Narrative montage: the cutting and ordering of shots to manipulate time and space.
- Ideational montage: images linked or juxtaposed together to create an idea.
2. How does montage progress the narrative?

TRENDS

The direction in which something is headed.

- Trends in representation, particularly of minority groups and women. Trends in representation on our screens have seen more TV shows and movies reflecting the fabric of diversity within society.
- Trends in technology use.
- Trends in aesthetic consideration such as the manipulation of narrative structure or codes and conventions.
- Trends in content or genre.

AGENDA SETTING

McCombs and Shaw posited that the media can't tell the audience what to think, but they can tell them what to think about.

Framing refers to what information is selected or emphasised, and what is omitted to 'frame' or compose content.
- Priming refers to the time, space and coverage provided to an issue, making some issues prominent and ignoring, or giving minimal coverage, to others.
- Gatekeeping refers to people, such as a news editor, who decide (through selection and omission) the content of media publications.

SELECTION & OMISSION

Selection and omission results in a bias, constructing media content is not neutral, privileging of characters, viewpoints, values, and ideologies will result in a particular idea or issue being foregrounded.

State what has been selected, what omitted?
- Selection – prioritising certain issues over others
- Emphasis – highlighting an issue, possibly through repetition. e.g., how many days does an item stay in the news cycle?
- Exclusion – omitting items from the agenda.

These terms, commonly associated with the Agenda Setting Theory.

GENRE

A genre is a category or classification into which media productions fall.

1. State the genre. Discuss the iconography that signals which genre the film belongs to.
2. Discuss audience expectation of the plot structure and events depending on the genre. Have these been supported or challenged?
3. Stephen Neale's theory of repetition and difference posits that the audience requires repetition for familiarity, however difference is required to maintain continued interest in the genre. Discuss any differences/familiarity.

WRITTEN CODES

Written codes anchor meaning to content.

- State the title and its connotation.
- Discuss any captions, headlines, speech bubbles or credits which relay meaning.
- Discuss the typography choice. What font and colour has been used to signal meaning in terms of genre and potential content?

DOCUMENTARY TECHNIQUES

How do the chosen conventions privilege the filmmaker's point of view?

State the techniques and its effect
- voice over
- testimonials and interviews
- archival footage
- re-enactments
- juxtaposition
- exposition
- authority figures
- statistics
- selection, omission, emphasis

SETTING

Defines the time and place in which the narrative occurs.

1. State the place and time
2. How does the place progress the narrative or set boundaries around what could occur within the narrative?
3. How does the time/era facilitate aspects of the narrative such as representations, use of symbolic and audio codes …?
4. Think about how the time/era links to contextual issues which may impact the narrative.

AUDIO CODES

Audio codes can be diegetic or non-diegetic, either originating from a source within the film, such as dialogue or atmospheric sounds to assist in the suspension of disbelief; or originating from outside the film world, such as the musical score or voice-over which anchors meaning to mood and content.

1. Discuss the connotations associated with specific dialogue (including accent and vocabulary choice). How does it establish character traits and progress the plot?
2. Discuss the connotations of music, sound effects and silence. What mood is established?
3. Discuss the use of voice-over to anchor meaning to the visuals.
4. Consider volume, pitch, rhythm.

AUTEUR

An auteur is someone whose films show a signature style, technically and thematically across a body of work. An auteur can be a director, screenwriter, producer, cinematographer, editor, music composer, costume designer, actor, production designer, or even a studio - the defining characteristic is that their filmography shows a clear and recognisable stylistic or thematic signature.

- What is the auteur's signature style? Give specific examples of codes, conventions and techniques used.
- Does the style reference conventions from film movements?
- Can you relate Andrew Sarris' privileging of the director to clear evidence in your text? Sarris posited that technical quality, personal style and interior meaning, when used consistently and in unison, define a director as an auteur.

PROBLEMS WITH STEREOTYPING

How do the chosen conventions privilege the filmmaker's point of view?

→ Simplification arises due to the narrow choice of codes used as a short cut in meaning to construct a representation, thus leading to inaccuracy.
→ Selection and omission – what is excluded what is foregrounded? Representations privilege certain views, ages, ethnicities, genders and so on. Whose agenda is served?

SOCIAL OR POLITICAL COMMENT

Power of media content to influence an audience's beliefs, values, and ideologies.

1. State the comment being made.
2. Analyse the codes, conventions and techniques used to construct the comment.
3. Discuss selection and omission in relation to agenda.
4. Discuss how a social or political issue is reflective of its context.
5. Discuss the power of media content to influence an audience's beliefs, values, and ideologies, potentially setting the agenda.

NATURALISTION OF STEREOTYPES

The codes used to form stereotypes are repeated with frequency, making them the natural and accepted way to view the group. The naturalisation process makes it difficult, but not impossible to shift attitudes regarding the group.

1. State the stereotype, analyse the codes of construction.
2. Discuss how oversimplification leads to inaccuracy. The process of choosing and repeating a few codes to represent the entire group means that generalisation and simplification occurs, narrowing the frame of reference regarding the group.
3. Discuss the values embedded in the choice of codes.

PROPAGANDA

To propagate or spread ideas or information in a deliberate manner designed to influence other's beliefs, attitudes and behaviours about a cause, institution, or person.

1. State the idea or message being spread.
2. Discuss the codes used to position the audience to decode the preferred meaning.
3. Discuss the values and ideologies embedded.
4. Discuss the context, why is this message being spread?
5. Discuss the agenda behind the spreading of the information.

MANIPULATION OF SPACE

Film space is primarily manipulated through sound, montage, and mise-en-scène.

- → Sound from a source outside of the frame suggests the surrounding space and atmosphere.
- → Mise-en-scène assists the audience to suspend their disbelief and engage with the fictional film space. The director, working with the set designer, will use spatial elements such as props, setting, costume, colour, and acting performance to create the fictional film space.

MANIPULATION OF TIME

How events are ordered within the narrative.

- Real time vs. screen time.
- Compressed time - graphic match, transitions, fast motion, simultaneous time, jump cuts ...
- Expanded time - freeze frame, slow motion, replay, cutaways, repetition ...
- Time manipulation techniques - flash back, flash forward, dream sequence, long take ...
- Temporal order, duration, and frequency.

MAINSTREAM FILM

Mainstream films have wide appeal and cater to a large demographic. They tend to appeal to society's dominant values, therefore maximising potential for both success and profit.

1. State the intended audience.
2. Explain the preferred meaning of the text and link it to the dominant values of the primary audience.
3. Discuss a mainstream audience's expectations of narrative structure, genre, narrative elements, film grammar ...
4. Discuss the accessibility of content in terms of themes, social or political comment ...

PERSONAL EXPRESSION

Personal expression is linked to auteur theory but not necessarily across a body of work.

- Discuss the elements which signal personal expression.
- Discuss aesthetics.
- Consider the manipulation or use of art film codes and conventions,
- Consider experimentation or manipulation of narrative.
- Discuss context - personal expression regarding issues, beliefs and so on.

EDITING TECHNIQUES

Used to establish screen space and narrative time, leading the viewer to understand what is important within the narrative.

Conventions include, but are not limited to:
- the use of montage,
- continuity editing,
- eye-line match,
- manipulation of time and space,
- use of rhythm and pace.

ALTERNATIVE FILM

Alternate film refers to movies whose content and style provide an alternative to mainstream Hollywood formulaic commercial narratives. Most alternative and experimental films fall into the independent, non-commercial film category.

1. Discuss how the film provides an alternative to commercial media in relation to conventional topics, themes, subjects, points-of-view, and formal elements not found in the mainstream.
2. Discuss how alternate film exposes the rules and challenges traditional film grammar and structures.
3. Discuss the use of innovative aesthetics and manipulated narrative structure.

EXPERIMENTAL FILM

The filmmaker experiments with the medium, technology, style, and structure of the media work. Most alternative and experimental films fall into the independent, non-commercial film category.

- Discuss how the filmmaker experiments with the medium, the production process, or the structure of the work, without necessarily knowing what the outcome will be.

FUNDING

Funding is not a measure of a film's potential success. A high budget film requires a high return; therefore, economics dictates that it is safer to stay within genre and thematic boundaries to appeal to a large audience to make money. A low budget film is less risky financially, therefore risks can be taken in terms of content and structure.

- State the source of the film's funding.
- Discuss the amount of money available and whether this constrains, allows for innovation, or supports the production's goals.
- Discuss any agenda attached to the film's funding source.
- Discuss how funding impacts narrative, film grammar and theme
- Consider cost of technology, cast, crew, marketing, distribution, product placement ...

USES AND GRATIFICATIONS

Blumler, Katz and McQuail looked at what people do with the media, rather than what the media does to people, the underlying assumption being that an audience will use the media for a variety of reasons

- For diversion
- For personal relationships
- Personal identity
- Surveillance, information.

REINFORCEMENT THEORY

Joseph Klapper (1960) promoted the idea that audiences would be more likely to accept and support an idea if it already aligned with their pre-existing values and ideas.

The audience actively uses media by:
1. Selective exposure
2. Selective retention
3. Selective perception

BINARY OPPOSITIONS

Claude Lévi-Strauss posited the idea that binary oppositions are used in narratives to fuel audience engagement by creating contrasting characters and ideas.

1. Fundamentally, for conflict to exist in a narrative, binary opposites must be present. This creates an opposition between the forces of good and evil or hero and villain.
2. These oppositions are not neutral, they privilege one element over another.

TODOROV'S THEORY

Todorov's structuralist approach to narrative theory posits that stories follow a similar pattern consisting of five distinct stages.

1. Equilibrium
2. Disruption
3. Recognition
4. Repair
5. Reinstatement

Terminology

- Media terminology
- Command verbs
- General sentence starters and stems
- Transition words
- Ways to describe camera movement
- Ways to describe camera shots
- Ways to describe sound
- Ways to describe editing
- Terms to describe and analyse media

Terminology

Media terminology

The flash cards in the previous chapter covered essential content terms found in the syllabus. Once you are comfortable with the definition of each term you will need to incorporate it seamlessly into your responses. By consistently incorporating relevant terms into your answers, you will demonstrate knowledge of the essential content, increasing the probability of your grade rising.

The sentence stems and terms in this chapter are arranged under the headings of frequently encountered topics in Media. The list is not exhaustive, it is simply a curated selection of terms which may assist you when writing on the topics listed below:

- Narrative
- Codes
- Symbolic codes
- Audio codes
- Written codes
- Technical codes
- Context
- Representations and stereotypes
- Audience
- Values, ideologies
- Editing
- Conventions
- Form
- Television
- Theme
- Genre
- Aesthetics
- Trends
- Institutions
- Popular Culture
- General

Included in this chapter:
→ Command verbs to help you understand what a question is asking you to do.
→ General sentence stems to assist with answering questions.
→ Transition words to help you flow seamlessly from one sentence or paragraph to the next.
→ Words and phrases to help you describe camera movements, shots, sound and editing.

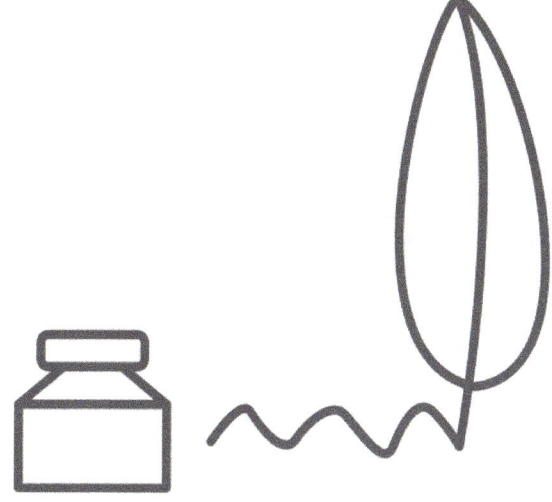

Terminology

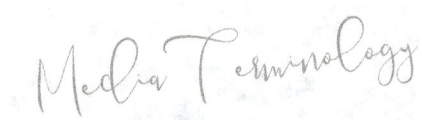

Narrative

- Genre expectations
- Point of view
- Goal of the protagonist
- Obstacles in the way
- Antagonist, protagonist
- The resolution draws the goal of the protagonist to a close by ...
- Narrative elements (character, setting, conflict and resolution)
- Narrative structure
- Todorov's structuralist approach (equilibrium, enigma, disequilibrium, return to equilibrium)
- Levi-Strauss' binary oppositions
- The inciting incident of x propels the action ...
- The exposition begins in equilibrium ...

Narrative

- A return to equilibrium occurs ...
- Attempts at repair ...
- Narrative construction
- Plot progression point
- Narrative story element of point of view
- Deviation from a traditional cause and effect narrative
- Manipulation of narrative structure
- Manipulation of time and space
- Quest
- Denouement
- Character subjectivity
- Character driven

Narrative

- Temporal order, duration, frequency
- Temporal sequencing
- Temporal experimentation or manipulation
- Narrative sequence
- Narrative puzzle
- Narrative progression points
- Narrative closure
- Narrative enigma
- Narrative pleasure
- Narrative possibilities
- Narrative plot progression plot
- Narrative premise
- Narrative clarity
- Binary oppositions
- Equilibrium, disequilibrium, enigma

Narrative

- Narrative structure
- Time manipulation techniques (flash back, flash forward, simultaneous time, split screen
- Spatial discontinuity
- Jump cuts - fracture the seamless continuity of time and space
- Narrative theory
- Traditional linear, cause and effect narrative
- Elliptical narrative
- Narrative information
- A disruption occurs
- Progresses the narrative
- Narrative goal
- Point of view constructs the narrative by

Terminology

Technical codes

- A point of view shot
- The extreme close up on x foreshadows y
- Lighting conventions of x create y connotation
- The handheld camera technique creates a sense of realism by
- A high camera angle connotes
- A wide shot contributes to a feeling of
- A close up reveals
- The harsh lighting suggests
- The camera dollies to reveal
- The 360° camera movement is coupled with
- Low key lighting
- The setting is anchored via a long shot of

Symbolic codes

- The symbolic code of colour used as a short cut in meaning to convey
- Colour palette, over saturation, under saturation
- Colour choice of x connotes y
- Mise-en-scène
- Clothing of x is used to represent y
- Setting conveys
- Clothing is representative of
- Object of x is used as a visual signifier of y
- Body language can be decoded as
- A combination of setting and colour suggests x about

Audio codes

- Diegetic, non-diegetic sound
- Aural motif, signifier
- Ambient sound
- Sound bridge
- Dialogue delivers character traits, specifically
- The opening dialogue of x positions the audience to
- The aural signifier of x suggests y to the audience.
- Mode of address
- Colloquial language
- Sound effects
- Mood creation
- Synchronous sound
- Asynchronous sound

Written codes

- Viewed through the lens of the caption
- The title functions to
- The title sequence employs
- Objective or subjective content
- The discourse employed suggests
- Word choice embeds the value of
- The headline functions to
- The typography choice gives visual and context clues to the audience by evoking
- Font choice creates the connotation of
- The written code of x positions the audience to decode y meaning
- Anchors meaning

Terminology

Codes

- Preferred meaning is shaped by the choice of codes
- Codes combine to form meaning
- Connotations of x code
- Meaning of x is constructed through the choice of y codes
- Visual signifier
- Choice of codes makes a value judgement by
- Meaning is encoded using the conventional visual signifier of
- Suspension of disbelief
- Diegetic world of the narrative
- Deconstruct the preferred meaning of
- Selection processes
- Codes are building blocks

Context

- Contemporary context
- Social landscape
- Cultural, economic, historical, social, and political contexts
- Contextual elements
- Context will always affect content
- Audience's previous contextual knowledge
- Contextual understanding
- Context clues
- Production context
- Reception context
- Cultural zeitgeist
- Cultural discourse
  - Cancel culture

Representations and stereotypes

- Representations disseminate understanding
- Naturalisation of stereotypes depart from, challenge, subvert, conform to, support
- Representations are value laden
- Oversimplification of a stereotype
- Perpetuated stereotype
- Naturalisation of stereotypes
- Codes of construction
- Stereotypical short cut in meaning
- Simplification in stereotypes leads to inaccuracy
- Stereotypes do not remain static, they change to reflect their cultural norms, specifically
- Dialogue facilitates stereotypes by
- The familial representation

Representations and stereotypes

- The setting furthers the representation of
- Representations privilege certain views
- Representations can control the construction and circulation of meaning
- Ideologies and values embedded in representations are
- The effect of stereotyping
- Stereotypical representations
- Stuart Hall's shared cultural map
- X is constructed to represent
- Choice of visual codes is representative of
- Normative representation
- Shift in representation
- Stereotypes use observable traits such as

Terminology

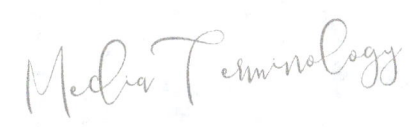
Media Terminology

Audience

- Mainstream audience
- Niche audience
- Primary, secondary, tertiary audience
- Narrowcasting vs. broadcasting
- Audience demographics, geographic and psychographic elements
- Demographic metrics
- Identifiable audience segment
- Target audience
- Intended audience
- Audience expectation
- Audience needs
- Marketing
- Active or passive audience
- Decode the preferred meaning

Audience

- Communication theories scaffold how an audience interprets a text
- Dominant, negotiated or oppositional audience interpretation
- Filtering factors
- Subcultural audience
- Palatable to the mainstream
- The intended audience engages with the content by
- A primary male, adult audience
- The intended adult western audience

Values, ideologies

- Value judgement
- Circulate beliefs
- Ideological messages
- Values revealed in the narrative's resolution are...
- Values embedded in the protagonist are
- Values and ideologies are circulated via representations
- Choice of codes of construction makes a value judgement
- Support, challenge or subvert ideologies
- Dominant values and ideologies
- Emerging ideology
- Oppositional values and ideologies
- Progressive ideology
- Value of x suggested by y action

Values, ideologies

- Ideology and representations are intertwined
- Disseminating ideology
- Underpinning ideology
- X character embodies the value of y
- Endorses the value of
- Ideological contest
- Reinforces ideologies
- Entrenched values
- Ideological viewpoints
- Carrying ideological meaning
- Oppositional discourse
- Discourse

Terminology

Editing

- Spatial discontinuity
- Jump cuts fracture the seamless continuity of time and space
- Pace, mood, rhythm
- Montage
- Temporal duration
- Cutting, cross cutting
- Audio bridge
- Match cut
- Continuity
- Eye-line match
- Match on action
- Graphic match
- Parallel editing
- The use of x transition suggests y

Conventions

- As conventions are expected ways of using codes
- The genre conventions of
- Conventional story telling structures create an expectation of
- The conventional use of x is manipulated by y
- Subvert the convention of
- The lighting conventions of the romance genre
- The villain is encoded using conventional visual signifiers of
- Conventions of realism consist of

Form

- Form affects content
- Form refers to how the content is shaped and considers elements such as the medium used (film, TV, podcast, YouTube short etc.), the narrative structure, the agenda of the institution making the production and audience expectations
- Linear television's form includes devices to engage the audience including immediacy, narrative complexity, segmentation, repetition, novelty, flow, and open-ended resolution
- Mainstream film's form includes

Television

- Linear vs. non-linear
- Ratings
- Scheduling
- Planned flow
- Segmentation
- Familiarity
- Repetition
- Subscription-video-on- demand or S.V.O.D.
- Over-the-top streaming or O.T.T.
- Video-on-demand or V.O.D.

Terminology

Media Terminology

Theme

- Main message
- Unifying concept
- Theme conveys the intention of the story
- Characters represent theme by
- The setting reveals the theme of
- The resolution communicates the theme by
- The codes of x, y and z convey the theme through
- Genre conventions of x convey the theme of y
- The narrative's stance on a topic expresses the theme, for instance
- The theme is exemplified by the visual signifiers of

Genre

- Iconography, motifs, symbols
- Genre conventions of
- Recognisable conventional character trait
- Audience expectation of narrative structure is reinforced (or challenged) via the use of
- The predictability of genre conventions allows for
- x code assists to establish the genre by
- Stephen Neale posited a theory of repetition and difference seen in
- Genre expectations
- Audio codes such as suspenseful music contributes to the thriller genre by
  - Lighting allows for the quick establishment of the horror genre by

Aesthetics

- Auteur signature style
- Filmography
- Style and form
- Intention and reception
- Distinctive style
- Visual aesthetic
- Sound as an aesthetic device
- Visual and aural motifs
- Pastiche
- Manipulation, experimentation, innovation
- Codes and conventions
- Creative intent
- Distinctive colour palette
- Aesthetic intention
- Artistic vision

Aesthetics

- Visual style, techniques used
- Subversion of Hollywood paradigm
- Niche audience
- Rejection or experimentation with film grammar
- Active audience
- Manipulation of narrative structure
- Open-ended resolution
- Deviation from realism
- Rhythm and pace
- Homage
- Film movement conventions
- Arise out of cultural context
- Inclusion of social or political comment
- Manipulation of time and space

Terminology

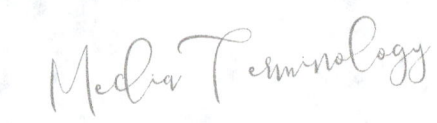

Trends

- Digital disruption
- Creator, influencer, prosumer
- Web 3, fourth Industrial Revolution
- Non-fungible tokens or NFT
- Non-linear
- Echo chamber, filter bubble
- Bots, trolls, data mining
- Misinformation, disinformation, fake news
- Globalisation
- Interactivity, immersive
- Curated, personalised content
- Virtual and augmented reality
- Pay wall
- Artificial intelligence
- Streamed content

Institutions

- Commercial, public, community service
- Funding
- Agenda
- Media monopoly
- Concentrated ownership
- Cross-media ownership
- Watchdogs
- Media reach
- Public relations press releases
- Regulatory bodies
- Legal and ethical constraints
- Production and technological constraints
- Censorship, classification
- Audience expectations

Popular culture

- Mass popularity
- Accessible, evolving
- High culture
- Mainstream culture
- Counter-culture
- Subculture - signal their belonging to a group through a shared identity
- Shaping popular culture
- Popular cultural issues
- Institutional/corporate culture
- Geographic/ethnic culture
- Generational culture

General

- Sense of immediacy
- Polysemic
- Opinion leaders
- Media diet
- Deconstruct
- Manipulates realism
- Selection and omission
- Juxtaposes
- Point of view
- Parody, satire
- Suspension of disbelief
- Trope
- Cultural imperialism

Command verbs

Questions in an exam or assessment will start with a **command verb.** Words like define, analyse, discuss, compare, evaluate and so on, are the words which signal what is expected of you when answering a question.

For instance:

1. **Discuss** how technical codes shape meaning in a narrative.
2. **Analyse** how a narrative is structured to engage an audience.
3. **Examine** the relationship between text and audience.

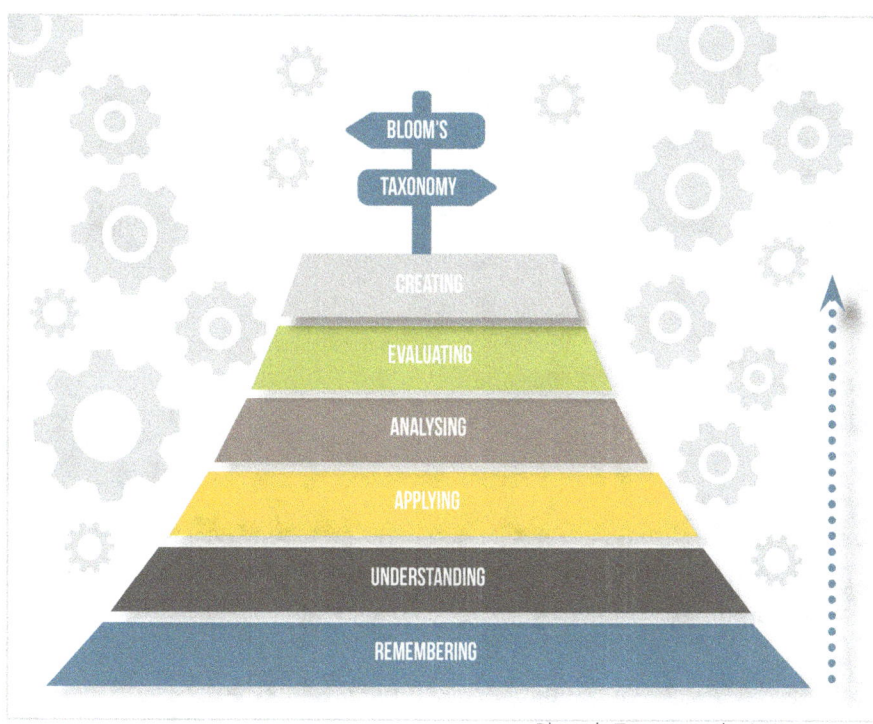

Bloom's Taxonomy depiction

Command verbs tend to be hierarchical in signalling the depth and detail required in an assessment. A scale of observable skills and knowledge was originally developed in 1956 by Benjamin Bloom and is referred to as Bloom's Taxonomy. The observable skills can be visually represented as a triangle with the most difficult skill at the peak. The taxonomy has undergone several iterations with the most recent being in the early 2000s conducted by Lorin Anderson and David Krathwohl who revised Bloom's Taxonomy to reflect an active teaching and learning environment.

Command verbs

Some common command verbs and their definitions are listed below. It is important that you read the command verb and understand what it is signalling to you in terms of the depth of your response.

Define: outline what the term means and how it functions. Support with specific textual examples.

Explain: provide clarity on a topic. Explanations require detail. Give clear reasoning supported with specific examples.

Describe: to give an in-depth description which provides clarity or understanding about the characteristics of the topic. Support with textual evidence.

Discuss: to look at different aspects of the text, exploring the pros and cons in a detailed manner. Support with specificity of textual evidence.

Examine: a detailed and critical examination of a topic. Pros, cons, strengths, limitations, and context are some aspects to consider and support with extensive evidence from the text.

Compare & contrast: a comparison of two or more texts. Identify differences and similarities. Explain the impact of these differences and similarities. Support with detailed textual evidence.

Analyse: to deconstruct a text, supported with detailed textual evidence.

Justify: must have an informed argument with relevant detailed evidence. Briefly include counter argument.

Evaluate: similar to discuss but has a judgement attached such as determining the strengths and weaknesses of a text. Include the argument and counter argument. Support with detailed evidence.

Critically evaluate: state a position on an argument. Depth of deconstruction required. Specificity and variety of evidence is needed to support claim. Provide alternative argument.

Command verbs

Bloom's Taxonomy

Media Production and Analysis response questions tend to use the command verbs in bold below. Discuss, analyse, compare, evaluate, and critically evaluate appear with frequency in the external exam. Make yourself familiar with these terms and what they are asking you to do.

BLOOM'S TAXONOMY TERMINOLOGY

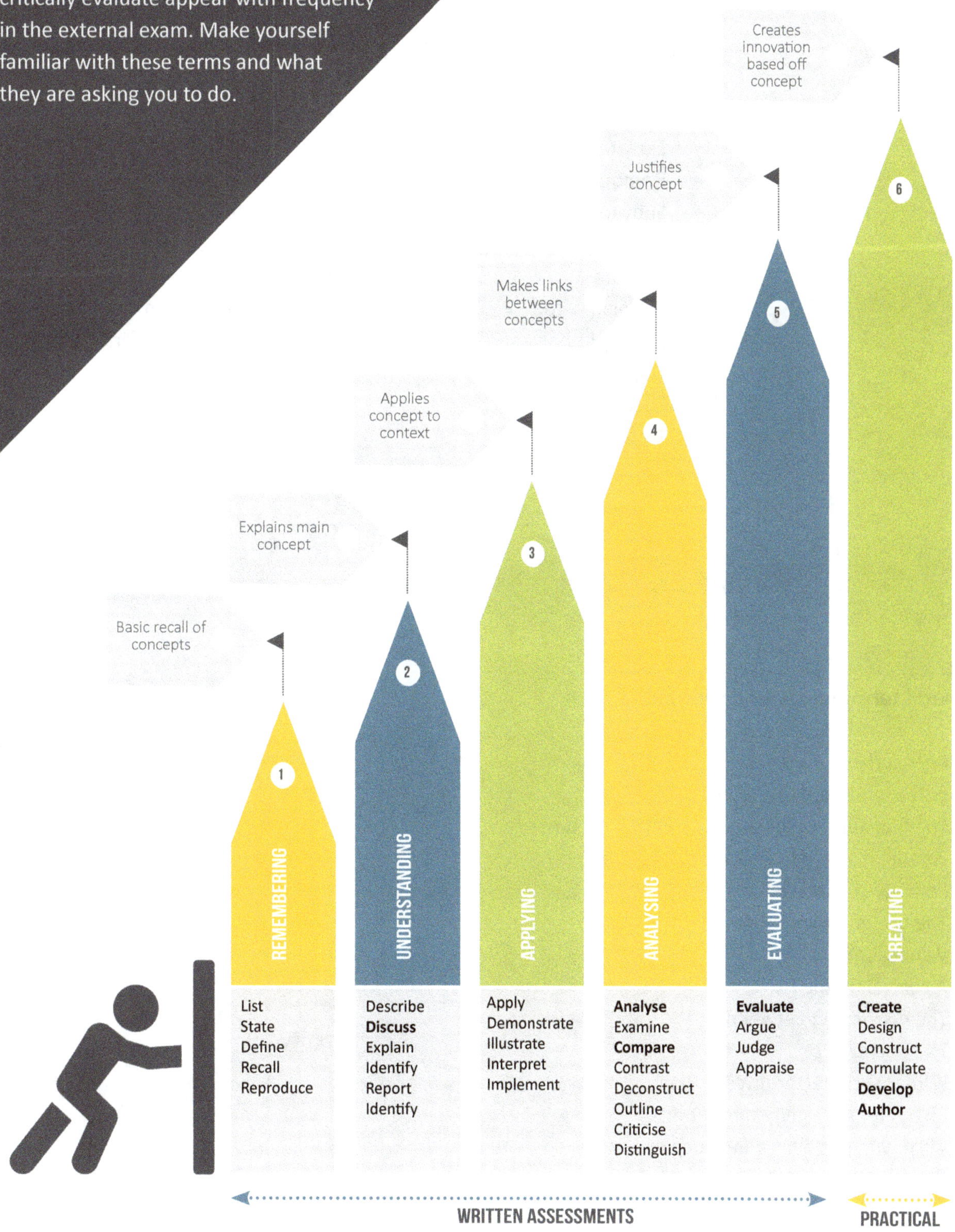

- 1 — Basic recall of concepts — **REMEMBERING**
- 2 — Explains main concept — **UNDERSTANDING**
- 3 — Applies concept to context — **APPLYING**
- 4 — Makes links between concepts — **ANALYSING**
- 5 — Justifies concept — **EVALUATING**
- 6 — Creates innovation based off concept — **CREATING**

REMEMBERING	UNDERSTANDING	APPLYING	ANALYSING	EVALUATING	CREATING
List	Describe	Apply	**Analyse**	**Evaluate**	Create
State	**Discuss**	Demonstrate	Examine	Argue	Design
Define	Explain	Illustrate	**Compare**	Judge	Construct
Recall	Identify	Interpret	Contrast	Appraise	Formulate
Reproduce	Report	Implement	Deconstruct		**Develop**
	Identify		Outline		**Author**
			Criticise		
			Distinguish		

WRITTEN ASSESSMENTS — PRACTICAL

General sentence stems

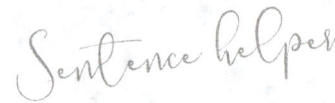

General Sentence Starters & Stems

- Focuses on
- Explores
- Demonstrates
- Subverts
- Encourages the audience to
- Examines
- Coupled with
- Equally important
- Together with
- In contrast
- To challenge
- Firstly
- To begin with
- Notwithstanding
- To enumerate
- In particular
- To demonstrate
- In the same fashion
- As an illustration
- An equally significant factor
- In addition to
- Comparatively
- By the same token
- To portray

General terminology and sentence stems

- Agency/lack of agency
- Purposefully appropriates
- The film appropriates the narrative structure of
- Paradigm (e.g. damsel-in-distress paradigm)
- Embody (x character embodies x values)
- The use of x allows for y
- Value laden
- A central theme
- The disconnect between
- The portrayal of
- Primarily character driven
- Character x is signified by y traits
- Align with positive values such as

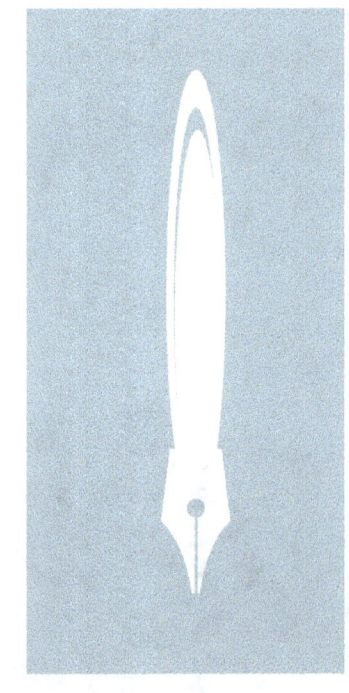

Transition words

Continuation
- additionally
- in addition
- further
- moreover
- as such
- equally important
- besides

Effect, consequence
- thus
- as a result
- hence
- this suggests that
- accordingly
- consequently
- resulting from
- therefore
- to this end

Time, sequence
- initially,
- subsequently
- while
- presently
- simultaneously
- at that time
- before
- formerly
- meanwhile

Examples
- namely
- for instance
- including
- for example
- specifically
- to illustrate
- such as
- to exemplify
- as evidenced by

Emphasising
- significantly
- specifically
- markedly
- in particular
- notably
- most importantly
- especially
- to demonstrate
- to clarify

Comparing
- in the same way
- similarly
- likewise
- equally
- instead of
- whereas

Contrasting
- by contrast
- alternatively
- conversely
- besides
- different from
- despite
- nevertheless
- in spite of
- although

Concluding
- in summation
- to summarise
- in essence
- as has been noted
- in brief
- as can be seen
- it can be concluded that
- in other words

Ways to describe camera movements

Sentence Helper

Describing how the camera movement is motivated by the action

- panning left to right, or right to left
- static frame
- hand-held
- crane up, crane down
- tilt up, tilt down
- dolly
- zoom
- slider
- push in/out
- fast motion
- slow motion
- 360° turn
- 180° turn
- whip pan
- tracking
- pedestal
- steadicam
- aerial or drone shot

Adjectives to describe how the camera shows the shot

- the camera's slow pan disclosure reveals
- subjective camera
- restless camera
- meticulously crafted
- camera is used as a tool to focus the audience's attention onto
- the static camera renders character x to be
- the camera seeks out
- the push in camera movement loiters on
- the tracking shot propels the audience
- the long take tracking the protagonist establishes
- the 360° camera movement visually ascribes the emotion of
- the camera technique of x is used as a narrative device to reveal x
- x employs the camera technique of ... to imply
- creates tension through fast tracking immersive camera work
- camera technique of x elicits a response of
- the aerial tracking shot establishes
- camera technique of x creates visual motion of y

MEDIA TERMINOLOGY

Ways to describe camera shots

Sentence Helper

Describing how the camera frames the shot:

- symmetrical composition
- asymmetrical composition
- closed frame
- open frame
- point of view shot
- two shot, three shot
- over the shoulder shot
- deep depth of field
- shallow depth of field
- pull focus /rack focus
- high, low and eye-level camera angle
- close up, long shot, extreme close up, mid-shot
- foreground, background
- dutch or canted angle

MEDIA TERMINOLOGY

Adjectives to describe shot framing and camera movement

- tight shot connotes urgency
- loose shot is more casual, calm
- x is isolated in the frame
- the camera strays
- revealing
- energetic
- tightly framed
- closed frame
- wide frame
- unstable
- wide shot establishes x

- unsettling
- disconcerting
- posed
- disorientating
- dreamy
- ominous
- jerky
- frenetic
- controlled
- choppy
- balanced

Ways to describe sound

Sentence Helper

MEDIA TERMINOLOGY

Words to describe how the sound is incorporated into the narrative:

- dialogue
- sound effects
- music
- atmosphere or ambience
- music score
- diegetic sound
- non-diegetic sound
- room tone
- volume
- rhythm and timing
- pace
- parallel sound
- contrapuntal sound
- voice-over or narrator
- sound motif
- foreshadowing music
- leitmotif
- sound bridge

Adjectives to describe sound:

- lilting
- tranquil
- balanced
- crisp
- mellow
- detailed
- focused
- realistic
- enchanting
- engaging
- elevating
- bold
- smooth
- soft
- dynamic
- rhythmical
- harmonious
- dulcet
- noisy
- aggressive
- muffled
- piercing
- shrill
- mysterious
- edgy
- boisterous
- thunderous
- discordant
- echoing
- pounding
- roaring
- howling
- insistent
- explosive
- hollow
- monotonous
- musical
- emotional
- silent
- dramatic
- speechless
- ambient
- artificial
- rasping
- faint
- clear
- comedic
- subdued
- low-pitched
- tunelessly
- inaudible
- sonorous
- tone
- plaintive

88

Ways to describe editing

Sentence Helper

Words to describe editing techniques:

- cut
- cross cutting/parallel editing
- continuity
- cutaway
- eye-line match
- establishing shot
- match on action
- jump cut
- split cut or L cut
- J or L cut
- montage
- shot-reverse-shot
- dissolve
- fade in/out
- iris
- wipe
- manipulating time
- flash forward/backwards
- freeze frame
- manipulating space
- smash cut
- match cut
- 180º rule
- pace, rhythm

MEDIA TERMINOLOGY

Describing how editing progresses the narrative:

- spatial continuity
- temporal continuity
- The opening shot of x immerses the audience in
- The cut to x reveals y about the protagonist
- The montage of x, y, z, suggests
- The sequence is intercut with x and y connoting
- Cut to the beat of the music to show
- Each cut is synchronised with
- The close ups of x are cut into the sequence to enhance the feeling of
- The execution of the editing, in particular the
- By juxtaposing x shot with y shot suggests
- The match cut is used as a visual connection to signal
- The smash cut of … highlights the theme of
- Faster pace accentuates tension and urgency, specifically
- The insertion of the point of view shot creates

89

Ways to describe editing

Sentence Helper

Describing how editing progresses the narrative:

- The jump cut of x conveys the movement of y
- Orienting the audience results from cutting between
- Cutting on the momentum allows for the frenetic pace of
- The extreme close up emphasises
- The sequence of the edit depicts
- Space outside of the frame occurs by including the sound of x to suggest
- The pace of the editing creates
- Continuity is created by
- The editing reflects the emotion of
- The eye-line matches between x and y creates a sense of space and reveals the facial expressions showing
- The editing effect of chroma keying
- Transitions such as fade in/out and wipe have been used to create the effect of time passing, specifically in the scene
- The dissolve into x is used to show y
- Spatial continuity is established by cutting to wide shots of … thus allowing for audience orientation that situates them in the environment of
- The special effects of … integrate well into the narrative and create realism by
- The editing technique of shot/reverse shot alternates between the characters of x and y revealing both sides of the conversation furthering the narrative regarding
- The music score supported the scene of x by connoting
- Seamless, invisible continuity style of editing is used to hide the cuts and allow the audience to suspend their disbelief
- Parallel editing adds suspense to the scene by
- The opening sequence distances the audience from the scene by
- In order to compress time, the montage of x
- The symbolism of x is created by using the editing effect of y
- Utilising an extreme long shot of x, followed by a close up of y connotes z
- The point of view shot aligns the audience with the protagonist by showing them
- The intertitle of x anchors meaning by explaining
- By utilising quick cuts x mirrors the film atmosphere of

MEDIA TERMINOLOGY

Terms to describe and analyse media

Describe & Critique

Terms to describe, analyse, and critique media products:

- Polysemic texts
- Mise-en-scene illustrates the
- X element foreshadows the
- The x code signals to the audience
- X non-diegetic music plays (in the background/at the start) positioning the audience to feel
- Media texts, such as X, can be influential in distributing and constructing values
- The incorporation of x code urges the audience to acknowledge/accept/reject the dominant/emerging/oppositional value of
- Camera techniques of x were employed to suggest/establish/highlight
- Camera movement of x communicates x
- The camera angle of x accentuates/diminishes
- The portrayal of x value is shaped by
- The use of x code/convention serves to
- Techniques such as use of an authority figure serve to
- The narrative includes a central character whose values/actions align with the target audience by demonstrating
- Use of written codes such as the slogan of x appearing on screen to anchor meaning
- X codes and conventions have a distinctly macho/feminine/youth appeal. As such shaping the ideology/value of
- Stereotype of x often promotes and naturalises y
- Subscribe to the values of the brand
- Masculinised environment
- Figures/characters are ambiguous, allowing the audience to place themselves
- Targeting an affluent market by
- The elements of ... create a unified message of
- Monochrome nature of the image suggests
- The lighting conveys
- The relentless action sequence is cut on movement, specifically
- Cross cutting between x establishes simultaneous time
- By cutting to an extreme close up of x shows that

MEDIA TERMINOLOGY

Essay structure

- T.E.E.L structure
- Formatting quotes
- Structure strips

Essay Structure

Essay structure

How to format

The point of writing an essay is to clearly answer a set question by forming a logical, structured, coherent argument. There are arguments for and against essay structures such as the T.E.E.L model provided on the following pages. Rather than being prescriptive or formulaic, it would be beneficial to use essay structures as a base to build upon. Once you begin to feel more confident, then branch out by experimenting with your own structure.

Your essay structure is determined by three main elements:
1. The creation of a clear introduction which outlines your thesis. The thesis is the main idea or contention of the essay which must encapsulate the essential content contained in the question.
2. Your body paragraphs are ordered according to the logic and flow of your argument. Each paragraph must contain one clear point which connects with the thesis and clearly exemplifies the essential content outlined in the question.
3. Your conclusion restates your thesis, summaries the main points made in your body paragraphs, and clearly answers the essential content requested in the question.

The essay structure outlined in the following pages has the acronym T.E.E.L. which stands for **T**opic sentence, **E**xplain, **E**xample, **L**ink. There are many examples of essay structures to be found all over the internet. You might find that in school or university you are taught to use different models. The element they all have in common is that they provide you with a clear way to structure your response. Begin by using the scaffold and support provided by an essay structure such as the T.E.E.L model; once you feel comfortable with writing a clear thesis, having body paragraphs that explain and exemplify one main point, and writing a clear conclusion, then begin to experiment on your own. Essay structure is essential to the flow and clarity of content. To improve your grade, use the structure provided to build a firm base. As your grades improve, and your skills grow stronger consider experimenting outside of the given structure. You need to have a clear understanding of the structural rules before you begin to innovate or break them for effect.

Essay formula

 Start writing, no matter what. The water does not flow until the faucet is turned on.
— Louis L'Amour

T.E.E.L MODEL
- Topic sentence
- Explain
- Example
- Link

Introduction
1. Grab your audience's attention with an interesting opening.
2. Include the name of the text, director/author, and year of release/publication.
3. Include a brief synopsis of the text - two sentences maximum.
4. Thesis statement - explain the essential content to be covered in your essay.
   * Use the key terms found in the question.
   * Make sure your thesis is succinct in establishing the purpose of the essay.

Body Paragraphs
1. **T**opic Sentence - **one** main idea only per paragraph.
2. **E**xplain the essential content from the topic sentence in more detail.
3. **E**xample from text. Make it **very** specific.
4. **L**ink to the next paragraph or link back to the essential content being asked for in the question. How does your topic sentence address the question?

Conclusion
1. Restate your main idea or thesis statement.
2. Summarise all topic sentence information.
3. Never introduce new information in the conclusion.
4. Final sentence - what do you want to leave your reader with? Make it meaningful. Link it back to the original question.

Essay plan

Write your essay question here:

Grab a highlighter and highlight the essential content terms found in the question. These terms should be the MAIN terms which signal what your essay will be about.

Write a quick dot point list of key words or knowledge associated with the terms you've highlighted. What do you know about your subject matter?

Using dot points, plan out your essay following the T.E.E.L structure.

Thesis Statement

What is your contention or main idea? What do you plan to argue and how do you plan to argue it? BE CLEAR. You must DIRECTLY address the question being asked. Include the main essential content terms you highlighted above.

What key points are you going to include to support your contention? These key points will become the main idea for each body paragraph. This is the road map for your essay structure which should show a logical progression of ideas.

95

Body Paragraph 1

Topic Sentence – what is the **ONE** main idea of this paragraph? Ensure this idea clearly addresses the essential content item you highlighted in the question.

T _____

Explanation- expand on your topic sentence by developing your argument and further explaining the main point above.

E _____

Example – use a specific quote from the text, or you can paraphrase, but your example must support the key idea in your topic sentence and your overall contention. You **MUST** have evidence in EVERY body paragraph.

E _____

Link – to the question being asked and/or transition into your next paragraph.

L _____

Body Paragraph 2

Topic Sentence – what is the **ONE** main idea of this paragraph? Ensure this idea clearly addresses the essential content item you highlighted in the question.

T _____

Explanation- expand on your topic sentence by developing your argument and further explaining the main point above.

E _____

Example – use a specific quote from the text, or you can paraphrase, but your example must support the key idea in your topic sentence and your overall contention. You **MUST** have evidence in EVERY body paragraph.

E _____

Link – to the question being asked and/or transition into your next paragraph.

L _____

Body Paragraph 3

Topic Sentence – what is the **ONE** main idea of this paragraph? Ensure this idea clearly addresses the essential content item you highlighted in the question.

T

Explanation – expand on your topic sentence by developing your argument and further explaining the main point above.

E

Example – use a specific quote from the text, or you can paraphrase, but your example must support the key idea in your topic sentence and your overall contention. You **MUST** have evidence in EVERY body paragraph.

E

Link – to the question being asked and/or transition into your next paragraph.

L

Body Paragraph 4

Topic Sentence – what is the **ONE** main idea of this paragraph? Ensure this idea clearly addresses the essential content item you highlighted in the question.

T

Explanation – expand on your topic sentence by developing your argument and further explaining the main point above.

E

Example – use a specific quote from the text, or you can paraphrase, but your example must support the key idea in your topic sentence and your overall contention. You **MUST** have evidence in EVERY body paragraph.

E

Link – to the question being asked and/or transition into your next paragraph.

L

Body Paragraph 5

Topic Sentence – what is the **ONE** main idea of this paragraph? Ensure this idea clearly addresses the essential content item you highlighted in the question.

T

Explanation- expand on your topic sentence by developing your argument and further explaining the main point above.

E

Example – use a specific quote from the text, or you can paraphrase, but your example must support the key idea in your topic sentence and your overall contention. You **MUST** have evidence in EVERY body paragraph.

E

Link – to the question being asked and/or transition into your next paragraph.

L

Conclusion

Restate your thesis statement.

Summarise all key points from your body paragraphs.

Give the reader something to ponder, possibly a future direction, a prediction, or a recommendation. Do not introduce new content in your conclusion.

Note: Add in additional body paragraphs as required.

T.E.E.L structure

Paragraph structure

Use a **communication theory** to explain how an **audience** is positioned to interpret a media text.

Opening Paragraph
This is the road map that tells the reader exactly what will be covered in the essay. It must include the essential content terms from the question.

T.E.E.L MODEL EXAMPLE

Topic sentence
Contains the topic, or main idea for that paragraph.

Explanation
Expand on you main idea.

Example
Give very specific textual examples which support the one main idea in your topic sentence.

Link
Link back to the original question by using the required terms.

OPENING PARAGRAPH

The razor brand Gillette's advert *We Believe: The Best Men Can Be,* released on social media in January 2019 has (at the time of writing) been viewed close to 30 million times, polarizing its audience with as much controversy as praise. The advert attempted to reposition its **primary male adult audience** by utilizing the rhetorical question as a self-reflective device by asking 'Is this the best a man can get?' whilst being accompanied by visuals showing men and boys engaged in acts of bullying, fighting and harassment. The **Agenda Setting Theory** can be used to explain how the Gillette advertisement incorporates **framing, selection, emphasis and exclusion** to unintentionally polarize its consumers.

BODY PARAGRAPH 1

Maxwell McCombs, who further developed the Agenda Setting Theory in 1972 famously stated that the **'media can't tell the audience what to think, but they can tell them what to think about'.** Gillette has an obvious economically vested interest in selling its products. To do this it selected an **ideologically** contentious issue, the #metoo movement, to use as a platform to appeal to its primary audience and to tap into the social issue of gender equity. By having the audience think about this issue in relation to its product Gillette walked a fine line to engage belief-driven buyers whose values must align with Gillette's, or they risk the consumer boycotting their brand. The advert **emphasised** toxic masculinity by showing men engaged in bad behaviour such as sexual harassment, bullying and discrimination whilst the **camera tracked** down a line of men taking part in the traditionally male pursuit of barbecuing chanting, "Boys will be boys will be boys will be boys." Toxic masculinity and its effects have been selected as a trigger point, and Gillette positions itself, and the men who favour their brand, as saviours, people who **ideologically** align with the dominant values of equality, mutual respect, and fairness. These **values** are embedded in the **advert's resolution** as the audience is shown men questioning their friends who sexually intimidate women, men who are willing to break up fights and praising men who advocate for the strength of their daughters. In the wake of the controversy surrounding the advert Gillette has questioned what is so offensive about these **values**? The **Agenda Setting Theory** scaffolds how Gillette **emphasizes** certain bad masculine traits whilst **excluding** positive male behaviours.

Signal verbs

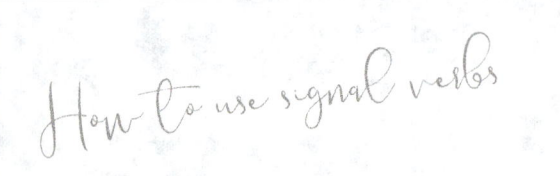

Your essay will occasionally need to quote directly from a source. Incorporating quotes can add credibility, provide evidence, and reinforce your argument. However, you must always give context to the quote. Do not simply drop it into a paragraph without first introducing it with a signal phrase or verb. Never leave a quote unexplained, always explain who the quote is from and clearly highlight how the quote supports the main point being made in your paragraph. A quote rarely appears at the beginning or end of a paragraph. It is embedded in the middle, bookended by a signal phrase which gives the quote context. Always include an interpretation which clearly describes how the quote supports your thesis.

ESSAY TERMINOLOGY

Some common signal phrases or verbs you can use to introduce your source quotations are listed below.

Choose a verb that matches the quotations stance - does the author argue for, or against, or is he/she stating a viewpoint. These verbs are not interchangeable. You must choose the verb that best fits your source's stance.

SIGNAL VERBS
used to signal your source's quotation stance

- X states
- X argues
- X reports
- X claims
- X explains
- X maintains
- X remarks
- X observes
- X discusses
- X points out
- X suggests
- X emphasises
- X notes
- X presents
- X declares
- X believes
- X comments
- X reveals
- X acknowledges
- X contends
- X endorses
- X predicts that
- X asserts
- X adds
- X addresses
- X speculates
- X admits
- X identifies
- X concludes
- X questions
- X reinforces
- X illustrates
- X compares
- X denies

SIGNAL PHRASES
which show your source's stance on the topic

- X demonstrates that
- X promotes the idea that
- X points out that
- X puts forward that
- In her article ------ X demonstrates that
- According to X
- X is credited with
- In his report, ------, X argues that

SIGNAL VERBS
which show you question the source

- X ignores
- X oversimplifies
- X disputes
- X refutes
- X denies
- X calls into question
- X challenges

Formatting quotes

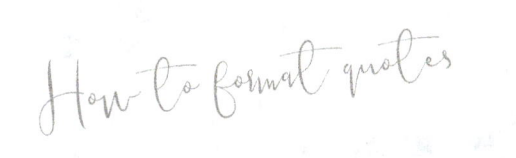

The use of quotation marks or in-text citation brackets signals that you are incorporating someone else's words or ideas into your work. By using correct quotation procedures, you will avoid being penalised for plagiarism.

Note that in exams full references are not required, however, if possible, an in-text reference to acknowledge the original author is a good idea.

Quoting a source in an essay varies according to the citation style required by your institution. Check which style is required as you can lose valuable marks by not using the specified citation style.

Citation styles dictate how to format referenced work. Common examples include:
- APA (American Psychological Association)
- Harvard
- Chicago
- MLA (Modern Language Association)

Why do you need to quote? By quoting you provide clear evidence to support your argument. Once you have supplied the quote you must explain, in your own words, how it supports your essay's contention. Never leave a quote unexplained.

You must always cite the original author whenever you use words or ideas that are not your own. Acknowledge and credit the original source, both in your essay, and in a reference list at the end of the essay.

You have plagiarised if you:
1. have not credited the original source
2. have not placed quotation marks around a direct quote
3. have paraphrased without supplying an in-text citation
4. have not submitted a bibliography.

Paraphrasing is when you read or listen to someone else's ideas and then write them down as your own without changing the substance of the text to reflect your voice. You cannot simply change a few words in a sentence from someone else's work and consider the idea yours. You can paraphrase when you supply an in-text citation which acknowledges the original source.

Direct quotes

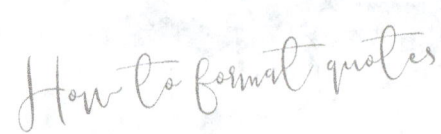
How to format quotes

Using APA 7th

Direct Quotes

If you plan to use the exact phrase from a book, newspaper article, magazine, journal, or use a specific line of dialogue from a film you need to:
- place quotation marks at the beginning and end of the phrase or sentence being used as evidence.

Example 1:

Episode one of season one of NBC's 1990 *The Fresh Prince of Bel-Air* tells the story of Will Smith, a sixteen year old boy whose mother forces him to leave his hometown of West Philadelphia to learn values and manners from his rich and successful aunt and uncle who reside in Bel-Air. Upon arrival Will comments on the scale of the house by comedically stating, "Man, next time I go to my room I'm gonna leave some breadcrumbs."

The quotation marks signal the exact dialogue spoken by the character of Will in *The Fresh Prince of Bel-Air.* The name of the show is referenced in text and therefore no need to include an in-text citation.

Example 2:

"Audiences are active participants in making meaning from media texts, not passive ingesters of content" (Merante 2022, p139).

The quotation marks signal the word-for-word replication of another person's work. The author's surname, year of publication and page number are positioned at the end of the direct quote. Note that the full stop sits outside of the parenthesis.

Example 3:

Quoting song lyrics - for instance Gambino sings:
"Yeah, this is America (woo, ayy)
Guns in my area (word, my area)
I got the strap (ayy, ayy)
I gotta carry 'em" (Glover, D., 2018, 1:19).

Surname of the artist, year of publication and timestamp showing where information was extracted from within the song.

In-text citation

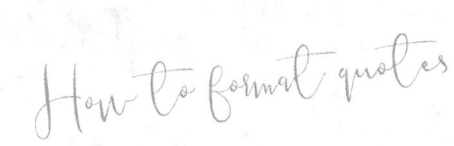

In-text Citation

Paraphrasing is used to include someone else's ideas into your work using your own voice. An in-text citation is needed to acknowledge the original source.

Merante (2022) points out that in *The Fresh Prince of Bel-Air* familial ideology is used to question historical notions of traditional family structure, privileging love and guidance over family unit construction.

Note, here the author's name forms part of the sentence, the year of publication is in brackets. This is known as a narrative citation as the author's name appears in the text. The full citation would appear in a reference list at the end of the essay.

The Fresh Prince of Bel-Air's pilot episode questions the familial ideology by privileging love and guidance over traditional family unit construction (Merante 2022, p130).

In this example the author's surname, year of publication, and the page number from which the information was extracted is cited in brackets after the paraphrased information. This is known as a parenthetical citation.

At the end of your essay supply a list of any sources you quoted or paraphrased. Note: this does not apply to exam essays or essays done under timed conditions.

Consider using a free citation generator such as:
- Bibme.org
- MyBib.com
- Citefast.com

It is always advisable to check the specific way your institution would like you to reference. Once you are aware of the style of referencing required, research the variables and perimeters to ensure compliance.

Structure strips

Using structure strips can assist in visualising and organising the elements required to write a cohesive, considered essay. By laying or pasting structure strips down on paper and writing dot points next to the required elements can assist in formalising thoughts on a topic. The concrete nature of seeing the essay points in writing allows for omissions to be seen and rectified. For instance, it becomes quickly apparent when you have not included a specific textual example, or not included one clear idea in your topic sentence.

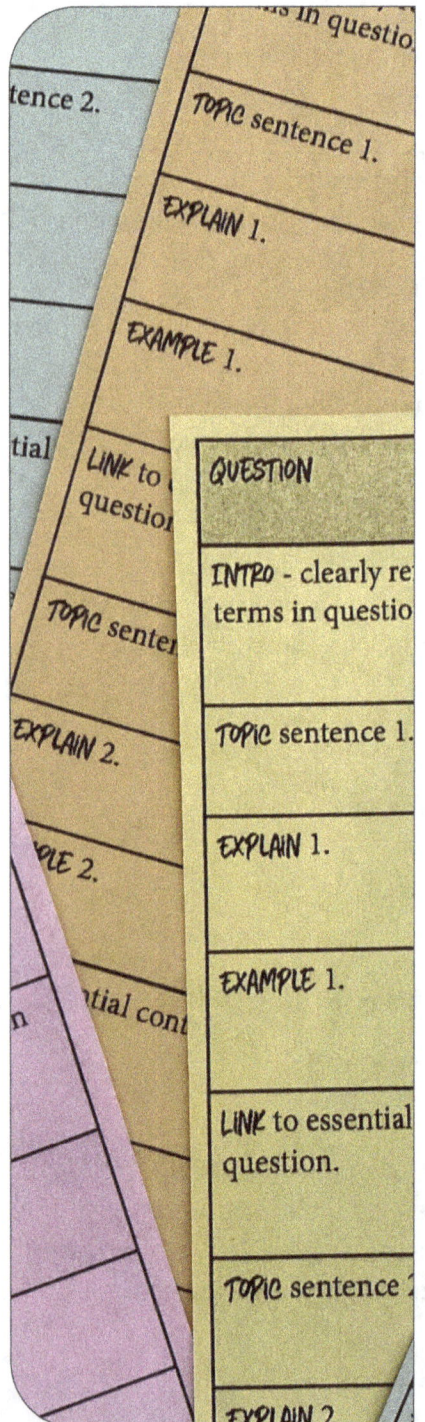

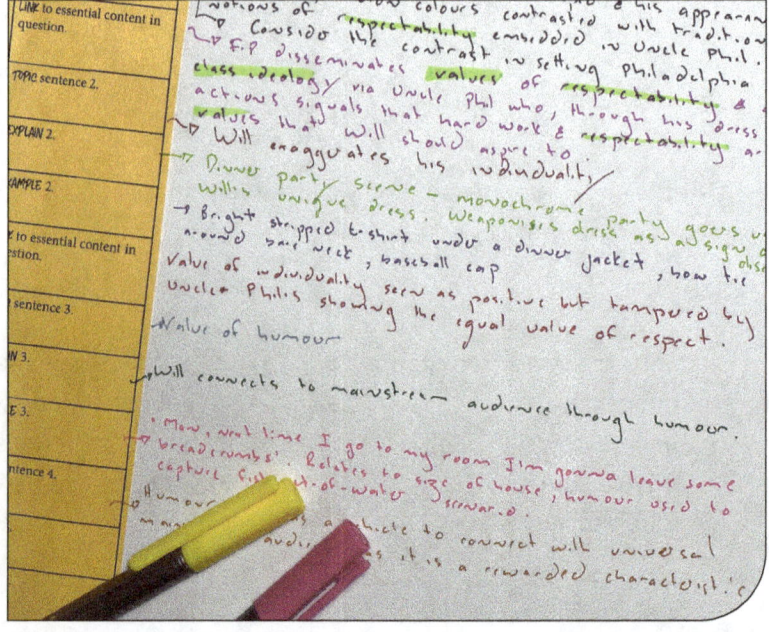

Essay planning structure

QUESTION	QUESTION	QUESTION	QUESTION
INTRO - clearly reference terms in question	INTRO - clearly reference terms in question	INTRO - clearly reference terms in question	INTRO - clearly reference terms in question
TOPIC sentence 1.	TOPIC sentence 1.	TOPIC sentence 1.	TOPIC sentence 1.
EXPLAIN 1.	EXPLAIN 1.	EXPLAIN 1.	EXPLAIN 1.
EXAMPLE 1.	EXAMPLE 1.	EXAMPLE 1.	EXAMPLE 1.
LINK to essential content in question.	LINK to essential content in question.	LINK to essential content in question.	LINK to essential content in question.
TOPIC sentence 2.	TOPIC sentence 2.	TOPIC sentence 2.	TOPIC sentence 2.
EXPLAIN 2.	EXPLAIN 2.	EXPLAIN 2.	EXPLAIN 2.
EXAMPLE 2.	EXAMPLE 2.	EXAMPLE 2.	EXAMPLE 2.
LINK to essential content in question.	LINK to essential content in question.	LINK to essential content in question.	LINK to essential content in question.
TOPIC sentence 3.	TOPIC sentence 3.	TOPIC sentence 3.	TOPIC sentence 3.
EXPLAIN 3.	EXPLAIN 3.	EXPLAIN 3.	EXPLAIN 3.
EXAMPLE 3.	EXAMPLE 3.	EXAMPLE 3.	EXAMPLE 3.
TOPIC sentence 4.	TOPIC sentence 4.	TOPIC sentence 4.	TOPIC sentence 4.
EXPLAIN 4.	EXPLAIN 4.	EXPLAIN 4.	EXPLAIN 4.
EXAMPLE 4.	EXAMPLE 4.	EXAMPLE 4.	EXAMPLE 4.
LINK to essential content in question.	LINK to essential content in question.	LINK to essential content in question.	LINK to essential content in question.
CONCLUSION summary of topic sentence info and link back to que.	CONCLUSION summary of topic sentence info and link back to que.	CONCLUSION summary of topic sentence info and link back to que.	CONCLUSION summary of topic sentence info and link back to que.

Graphic organisers

- Study flash cards
- Study booklet graphic organiser
- Codes graphic organiser
- Target audience graphic organiser
- Narrative elements graphic organiser
- Context graphic organiser
- Values and ideologies graphic organiser
- Stereotypes and representations graphic organiser

Graphic Organisers

Graphic organisers

Why use graphic organisers?

Graphic organisers are a visual tool used to organise content in a clear manner. The clarity of a well-designed graphic organiser can assist you to make links between concepts and recall information when required for assessments. You could choose to write your ideas in a long list down a page, however, by chunking or segmenting information in a graphic organiser you will optimise your learning as the content is organised in a clear framework which allows for ease of retention, recall and use. Graphic organisers can include sketches, graphs, charts, or any visual depiction to assist with visualising ideas and concepts, thus helping to make connections and allowing for retention of information.

Why use a graphic organiser:
- → visual framework clearly organises information into digestible segments
- → allows for linking of information to take place more clearly
- → the visual and chunked nature of information enhances recall and retention of content
- → segmenting information into categories simplifies it for ease of use.

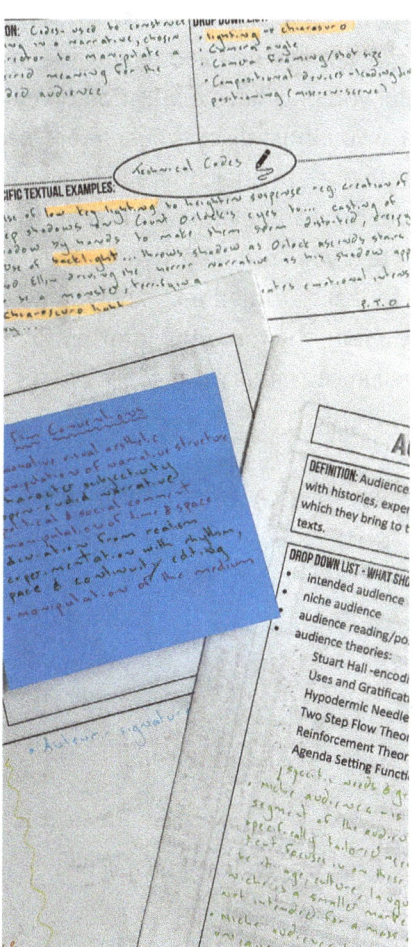
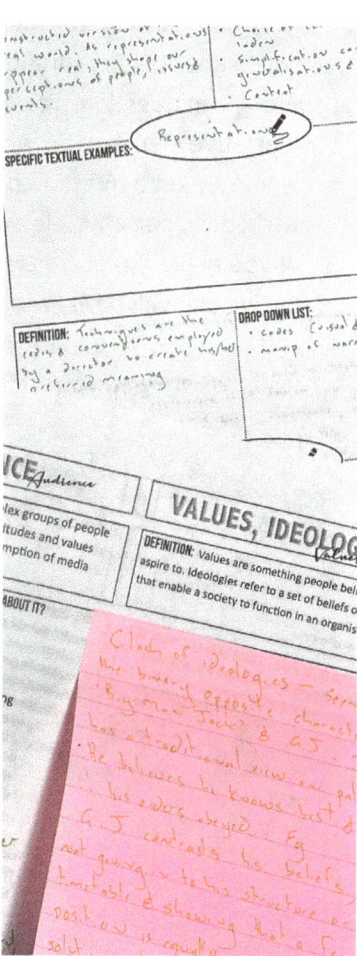

Study flash cards

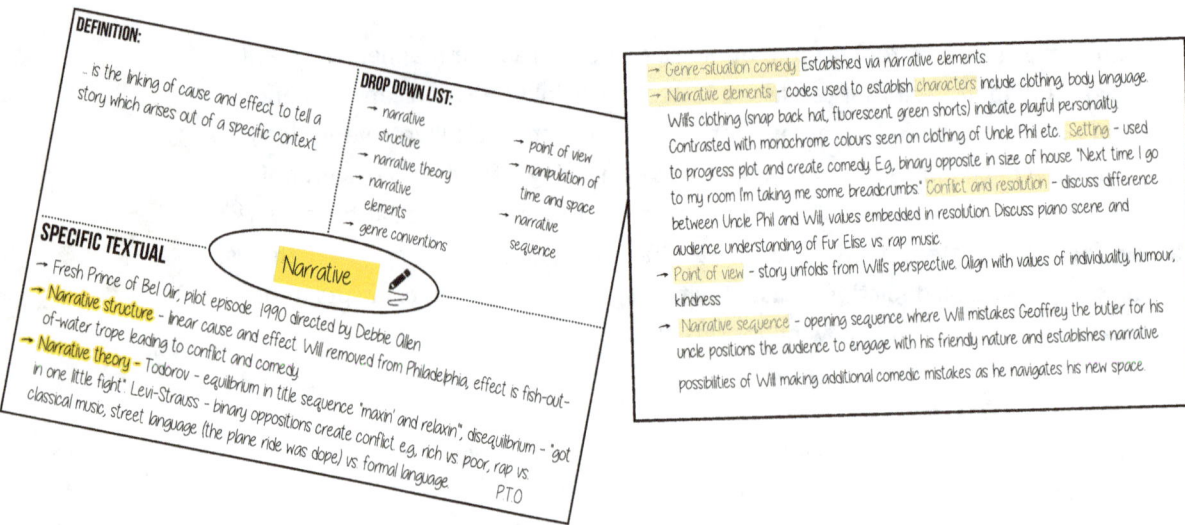

To assist with effective study for written timed assessments consider implementing the use of study flash cards which include specific textual examples pertinent to the text/s you have studied in class.

1. Begin by making a series of flashcards which contain the definition of the essential content term in the top left. The reason for writing down the definition is not for you to parrot it back to an examiner but to ensure you understand what the term means and when to use it appropriately.

2. The drop-down list is all the subheadings of information relating to the main essential content term which need to be considered when answering the question. This does not mean that you have to write about every sub-point, however, you do need to consider the aspects most suited to answering the given question. For example, you may have a question on narrative which asks specifically about narrative elements, in which case you must discuss characters, setting, conflict and resolution. Or, you may get a question on narrative techniques, this allows you to choose aspects such as narrative structure, narrative elements, genre, manipulation of time and space or point or view.

3. If you make flash cards for each text you study throughout the year, by the time your final exams arrive you will have flash cards for each studied text, and you would have used them for a few in-class assessments. The more you use them, the more the information will move into your long term memory thus assisting you to achieve well in your final exams.

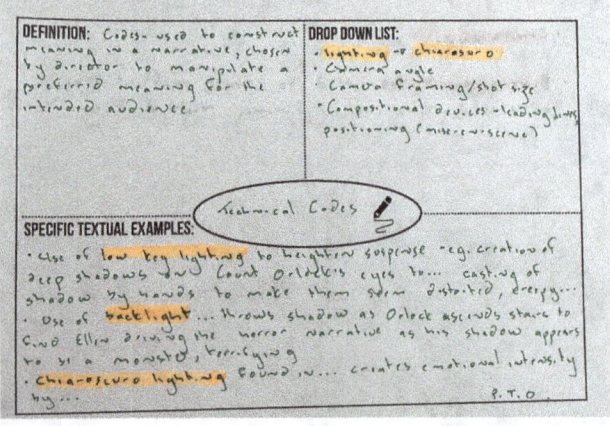

The following page contains a template for you to photocopy. Cut out the flash cards and use a bulldog clip to keep all the cards relating to a specific text together. If you can, I suggest you photocopy the template using different coloured paper. This way all of the information for one text is on one colour paper, all of the information for your second text on a different colour, making it easier to stay organised and assist with active recall.

Study flash card template

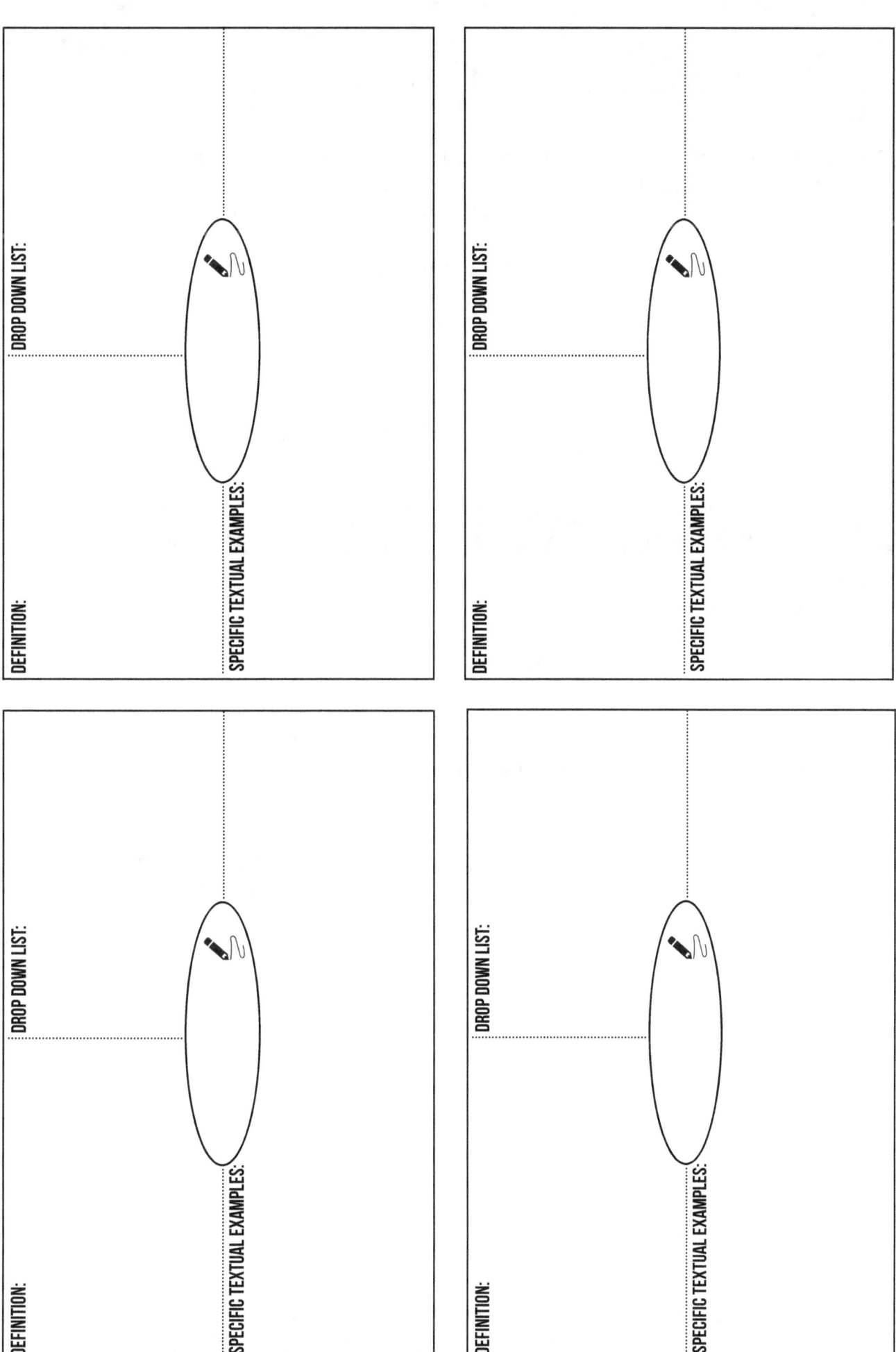

109

Study graphic organiser booklet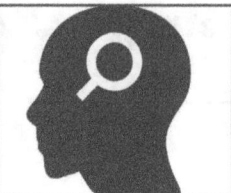

There are numerous ways to create effective, organised study habits. The previously mentioned flash cards work extremely well for some people. Other people need more information and therefore prefer to contain their study notes in a booklet. The following pages give you an example of how to organise the syllabus content using a booklet which contains:

→ headings for the major essential content covered in the course,
→ space to write down key terminology associated with the piece of essential content
→ space to write specific textual examples pertaining to the essential content
→ to add space to each section, use coloured sticky notes
→ Included are some template pages which do not have the essential content item written at the top. In Year 11 and 12 some areas differ. For example, in Year 11 you will cover popular culture but not in Year 12. This means you will have a few differences in the essential content covered over both years of the course. The following list is not exhaustive but can include:

YEAR 11 & 12 CONTENT	YEAR 11 CONTENT	YEAR 12 CONTENT
• Representation and stereotypes • Values and ideologies • Audience (mainstream and niche) • Subculture • Context • Narrative • Controls and constraints • Point of view • Trends • Communication theories • Narrative theories • Codes • Conventions • Production context • Commercial and independent media • Globalisation • Documentary techniques • Selection, emphasis, and omission • Encoding, decoding • Preferred, negotiated, oppositional meaning • Theme	• Popular culture • Realism • Classification and censorship • Journalistic media • Concentrated media ownership issues • Audience reach • Immediacy, accessibility • Influential media • Ethical and legal issues and their consequences	• Aesthetics • Auteur • Film movements - media in different times • Niche audience • Marketing, production, distribution and exhibition. • Persuasive techniques • Propaganda • Censorship • Dangers in naturalising stereotypes

Graphic organisers

Why use graphic organisers?

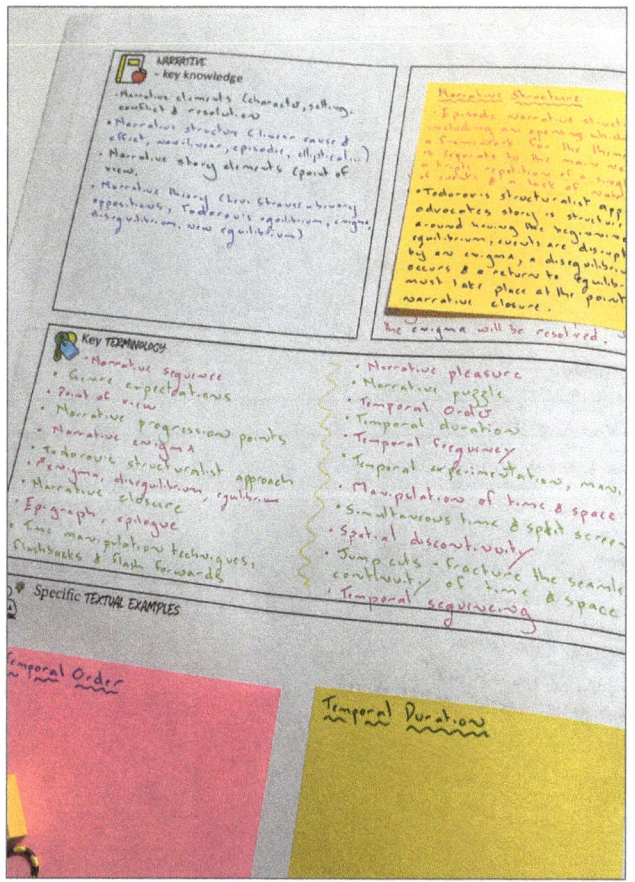
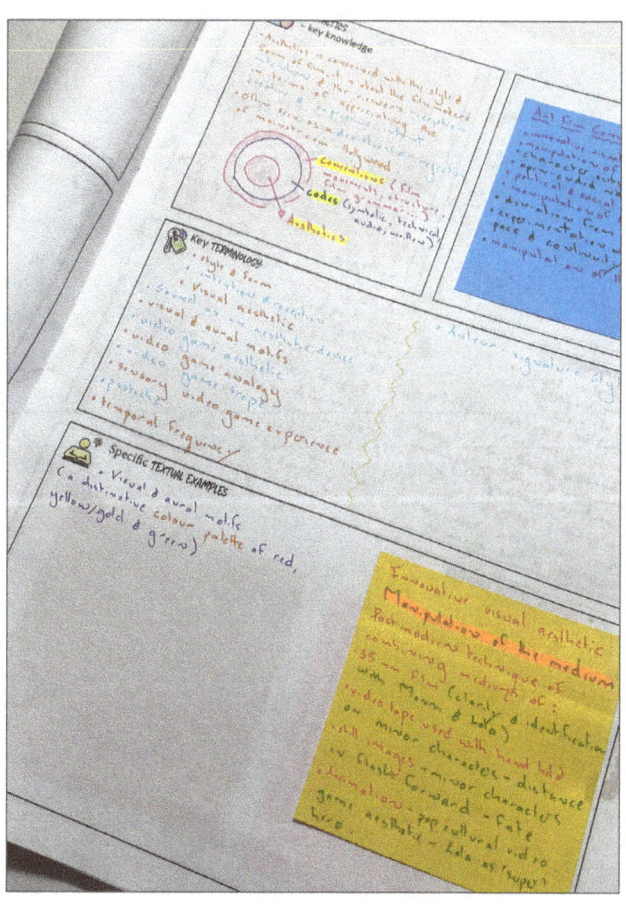

Instructions for use:
1. The following pages contain the essential content headings pertaining to both Year 11 and 12. Write directly into this journal or photocopy the main pages, and as many blank templates as needed; staple into a booklet to use when studying a specific text.
2. As you study a text complete small sections in the booklet to slowly build up to having a comprehensive study guide by the end of the course.
3. Add in any additional headings as you see fit based on the content in the syllabus, and exam or in-class assessments.
4. Remember that it does not always have to be prescriptive written text, but can be sketches, designs, storyboards, charts, or graphics to help you make the necessary connections for your revision.

REPRESENTATIONS & STEREOTYPES
Key knowledge

Key TERMINOLOGY

Specific TEXTUAL EXAMPLES

VALUES AND IDEOLOGIES
Key knowledge

Key TERMINOLOGY:

Specific TEXTUAL EXAMPLES

AUDIENCE: MAINSTREAM & NICHE
Key knowledge

Key TERMINOLOGY

Specific TEXTUAL EXAMPLES

SUBCULTURE/SOCIAL GROUPS
Key knowledge

Key TERMINOLOGY

Specific TEXTUAL EXAMPLES

CONTEXT
Key knowledge

Key TERMINOLOGY

Specific TEXTUAL EXAMPLES

NARRATIVE
Key knowledge

Key *TERMINOLOGY*

Specific *TEXTUAL EXAMPLES*

CONTROLS & CONSTRAINTS
Key knowledge

Key TERMINOLOGY

Specific TEXTUAL EXAMPLES

POINT OF VIEW
Key knowledge

Key TERMINOLOGY

Specific TEXTUAL EXAMPLES

TRENDS
Key knowledge

Key TERMINOLOGY

Specific TEXTUAL EXAMPLES

MEDIA THEORIES
Key knowledge

Key TERMINOLOGY

Specific TEXTUAL EXAMPLES

CODES
Key knowledge

Key TERMINOLOGY

Specific TEXTUAL EXAMPLES

CONVENTIONS
Key knowledge

Key TERMINOLOGY

Specific TEXTUAL EXAMPLES

COMMERCIAL & INDEPENDENT MEDIA
Key knowledge

Key TERMINOLOGY

Specific TEXTUAL EXAMPLES

GLOBALISATION
Key knowledge

Key TERMINOLOGY

Specific TEXTUAL EXAMPLES

DOCUMENTARY TECHNIQUES
Key knowledge

Key TERMINOLOGY

Specific TEXTUAL EXAMPLES

SELECTION, EMPHASIS, OMISSION
Key knowledge

Key *TERMINOLOGY*

Specific *TEXTUAL EXAMPLES*

ENCODING & DECODING
Key knowledge

Key TERMINOLOGY:

Specific TEXTUAL EXAMPLES

PRODUCTION CONTEXT
Key knowledge

Key TERMINOLOGY:

Specific TEXTUAL EXAMPLES

THEME
Key knowledge

Key TERMINOLOGY:

Specific TEXTUAL EXAMPLES

AESTHETICS
Key knowledge

Key TERMINOLOGY

Specific TEXTUAL EXAMPLES

PROPAGANDA
Key knowledge

Key TERMINOLOGY

Specific TEXTUAL EXAMPLES

PERSUASION TECHNIQUES
Key knowledge

Key TERMINOLOGY:

Specific TEXTUAL EXAMPLES

DANGERS IN NATURALISING STEREOTYPES
Key knowledge

Key TERMINOLOGY

Specific TEXTUAL EXAMPLES

MARKETING, DISTRIBUTION, EXHIBITION
Key knowledge

Key TERMINOLOGY:

Specific TEXTUAL EXAMPLES

Key knowledge

Key TERMINOLOGY:

Specific TEXTUAL EXAMPLES

Key knowledge

Key TERMINOLOGY:

Specific TEXTUAL EXAMPLES

Key knowledge

Key TERMINOLOGY

Specific TEXTUAL EXAMPLES

Key knowledge

Key TERMINOLOGY:

Specific TEXTUAL EXAMPLES

Graphic organisers

The graphic organisers on the following pages can be used to deconstruct texts. They can assist in organising your ideas on specific essential content prior to writing an assessment. Once you can see the information visually it makes it significantly easier to find specific textual examples which highlight your understanding of the relevant essential content. The next few pages contain graphic organisers for the following concepts:

CODES
A media producer will manipulate and choose specific codes: symbolic, written, audio and technical to create a **preferred meaning** for an intended audience. If you are asked to discuss the codes of construction for a given text then it is useful to break the codes up into their four areas, as well as the associated subsets. Do not attempt to cover every aspect of every code, focus on relevant aspects and discuss in detail.

TARGET AUDIENCE
The target audience is the intended audience for the message of the media text. To determine who the target audience is, look at the characters in the media text, the setting, the content, the codes used to construct it and most importantly, the marketing strategies. Who is the marketing primarily aimed at?

CONTEXT
Context refers to the background behind a fact, event, period, or the circumstances surrounding an event. Discuss the cultural context, including **relevant** historical, political, economic, and social contextual elements. All aspects of context intertwine. Always relate context to content in the text. Do not discuss every historical event that occurred in the year the text was produced. Only ever discuss contextual elements which are clearly **evidenced in the text.**

NARRATIVE ELEMENTS
The basic elements contained in narratives are **characters, setting, conflict and resolution.** These elements are the scaffold upon which the story and plot are built. When deconstructing the narrative elements consider:
- Recognisable character traits associated with the protagonist and antagonist. What values are suggested by these traits?
- How does the setting, which includes the time period and location, impact the narrative in terms of historical, social, cultural and political events?
- Discuss the conflict in terms of it being the central interest or theme within the narrative. Link the conflict to the goal of the protagonist, obstacles in the way and highlight the values embedded in the protagonist's goal.
- Values are revealed in the resolution of the conflict. Are good actions rewarded and bad punished?

Graphic organisers

Why use graphic organisers?

VALUES AND IDEOLOGIES
A **value** is a quality, something people aspire to and believe is worth striving for. **Ideology** is used to describe a shared system of beliefs, values and ideas which create a framework for organising and interpreting a culture. When analysing the role the media plays in disseminating values and ideologies in media texts consider the following:

- Who or what is **privileged** in the text? Consider factors such as gender, race, ethnicity, and age. What does this say about what, or who is **valued**?
- Deconstruct the **actions and appearance** of the main characters. What actions and appearance are attributed to the hero, heroine and villain? What symbolism is at play within their appearance? How might these symbols inform the viewers of the **values** and **ideologies** at play?
- Consider the **dialogue** of the antagonist versus the protagonist. How do they speak, what type of words are used - do they indicate education, ethnicity, or specific traits? What is **valued** and what is not?
- How is the **narrative resolved**? Does the traditional paradigm of good winning over evil prevail? For instance, is the **value** of justice and its supporting **ideology** of law and order supported, or is it challenged?
- Does the narrative **support** the status quo **or challenge** existing ideologies?
- What is the **dominant ideology** in the text? Whose **agenda** is served by this ideology?

STEREOTYPES AND REPRESENTATIONS
Representations in media texts re-present a filtered version of reality to the audience; it is not the real world but a mediated version of the world. Representations, when continually used, produce stereotypes as they use simplified, usually visual traits, as a short cut in meaning.

Main essential content to discuss when analysing representations and stereotypes:

- **Codes and conventions** – discuss how the choice of codes shapes the construction of the representation.
- **Simplification** – when a representation is continually used it produces a stereotype due to the simplified visual and aural traits being used as a short cut in meaning.
- **Selection and omission** – what is excluded, what is foregrounded? Representations privilege certain views, ages, ethnicities, genders and so on.
- **Context** – representations are not made in a vacuum; they are created within a set of cultural and social norms.
- **Values and ideologies** – representations are value-laden. Have positive or negative codes been chosen to represent the group?

Codes graphic organiser template

 **Symbolic**
- Costume
- Setting
- Objects
- Colour
- Body language, including facial expressions, hair, and make-up

 **Technical**
- Camera angles, movement
- Shot sizes, framing
- Lighting
- Shutter speed, lens choice, aperture
- Compositional devices - leading lines, rule of thirds, positioning ...
- Special effects
- Editing

CODES

 **Audio**
- Music
- Dialogue, including accent and vocabulary choice
- Sound effects
- Voice over narration
- Use of silence
- Consideration of rhythm, volume, pace and pitch

 **Written**
- Titles
- Credits
- Captions
- Speech bubbles
- Headlines
- Typography
- Font choice

Target audience graphic organiser template

socio-demographic

- gender
- age
- occupation
- ethnicity
- education (job type, level of income)
- religion

geographic

- country
- city
- urban
- suburban

psychographic

- lifestyle
- values, beliefs
- attitudes
- needs, wants, desires
- behaviour
- likes and dislikes
- interests
- opinions

For logistical and financial reasons, the **demographic, psychographic and geographic variables** need to be considered in terms of who the **primary, secondary, and tertiary audience** is.

Primary audience

Secondary audience

Tertiary audience

Narrative elements graphic organiser template

  **Elements**

 **Characters** — Deconstruct the appearance and actions of the protagonist and antagonist. What values are suggested by what they look like, and what they do?

 Setting — Setting reveals time and place. Consider the contextual elements which arise from time and place, how do they shape the narrative? What are the connotations associated with the setting?

 Conflict — Link the main conflict to the theme. What is the goal of the protagonist? What obstacles are in the way? Discuss the values embedded in the protagonist's goal.

 Resolution — Values are revealed in the resolution of the conflict. Are good actions rewarded and bad punished? How does the resolution reveal the theme?

Context graphic organiser template

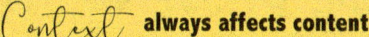 **always affects content**

Historical Context

Includes, but not limited to:
- wars
- inventions
- extreme weather events
- Civil Rights movement
- Feminist movement
- recession or depression
- religion ...

Social Context

Includes, but not limited to:
- language use
- entertainment
- education
- fashion
- employment trends
- food
- family structure ...

Political Context

Includes, but not limited to:
- political ideologies
- political propaganda
- political leaders ...

Cultural Context

Includes, but not limited to:
- gender roles
- religion
- family structure
- sexual orientation
- class or social status
- education and job opportunities ...

Values and ideologies graphic organiser

Analysing
VALUES & IDEOLOGIES

 When analysing the values and ideologies embedded in a media narrative consider:

1. Does the text promote, **challenge, reinforce, confirm, endorse** or **subvert** the dominant values and ideologies?

2. What values and ideologies are suggested by the **actions, appearance** and **dialogue** of the protagonist and antagonist?

3. Which representations are **foregrounded,** and which are **omitted**? What values are suggested by privileging specific representations?

4. What values and ideologies are embedded in the **conflict**? What is suggested to be worth fighting or striving for?

5. What values and ideologies are embedded or suggested by the **resolution**? Does good win over evil, is love found, is justice served …?

Representations graphic organiser

Analysing REPRESENTATIONS
STEREOTYPES &

Stereotypes are constructed from a choice of codes:
- the choice of codes is value laden
- repeated use of stereotypes causes naturalisation
- simplification associated with the choice of codes causes generalisations and errors associated with labelling an entire group.

1. Discuss how the choice of **codes** shapes the construction of the representation.

2. Representations are **value laden**. Have positive or negative codes been chosen to represent the group, issue, or event?

3. Representations privilege certain views, genders, ethnicities and so forth. What has been **omitted** and what **selected**?

4. Discuss how **simplification** leads to inaccuracy due to simplified visual and aural traits being used as a short cut to create meaning.

5. How has **context** affected the construction of representations and stereotypes?

Chapter Seven

Drop-down list of essential content

- Year 11 drop-down lists
- Year 12 drop-down lists
- Sample drop down list

Breaking down elements for each concept

Essential Content drop-down list

Each of the essential content syllabus points has associated information which informs and shapes your assessment responses. It helps to think of the related information in terms of a drop down list. The main essential content item sits at the top and all the associated content sits underneath. For instance:

DROP DOWN LIST
CONTEXT- always affects content.
- Consider the historical, social, political, and cultural context surrounding the text's production.
- Production context - when and where a text is made is different to where the text is set. Who made it? What is their agenda? Is the institution independent or commercial?

A drop-down list functions to categorise and organise information associated with a main topic. It gives the user a choice of relevant content to select from when writing on any given subject matter.

By learning and implementing the 'drop-down list' method you will chunk information into bite size pieces, making it easier for you to remember the relevant information associated with an essential content term. When you metaphorically open your drop-down list, you will have a wide selection of content to choose from when answering a timed question.

Your job is to choose and apply the relevant content from the 'drop-down' list. The major benefit of this method is that:

- Smaller chunks of information are easier to remember.
- In a timed assessment you are not sitting staring at a question unsure of how to answer it. Instead, you have trained yourself to read the question, find the main essential content items being asked for, such as 'representation', 'narrative', 'audience' and so on, then quickly jot down your drop-down list of elements; you now have the main information out of your head and onto the paper. You can turn your attention to choosing the appropriate elements from the drop-down list which are relevant to answering the question.
- You should not waste time in a timed assessment writing down absolutely everything from the drop-down list. Instead, write the main headings only. Once you have homed in on what aspects you think are relevant to successfully answering the question, then jot down the sub areas within your drop-down list. For instance, a question on codes and conventions would see me quickly jotting down the acronym S.W.A.T to remind myself of the four codes, then I would jot down some conventions pertaining to the text I planned to use as textual evidence. For example, if I planned to write on a documentary, I would jot down some documentary conventions, or if I planned to write on a TV show I would jot down the conventions associated with the medium of television.

Year 11 drop-down lists of essential content

The drop-down lists of essential content for Year 11 and Year 12 have some similarities and some differences due to the different contexts studied. Refer to the relevant year group to enhance your study.

 ## CODES

 ## CONVENTIONS

DEFINITION: Codes are used to construct meaning within a narrative. A director will manipulate and choose specific codes to create a preferred meaning for an intended audience.

DEFINITION: are the expected practices or established ways of using **codes and techniques.** They can be used to either subvert, challenge, or reinforce viewer expectations.

DROP DOWN LIST - WHAT SHOULD I KNOW ABOUT IT?
- Symbolic codes are:
    - costume
    - objects
    - setting
    - colour
    - body language, including facial expressions, hair, and make-up.
- Technical codes are:
    - lighting
    - shot size
    - camera angle
    - camera movement
    - compositional devices
    - shutter speed, aperture, lens choice
    - editing
    - special effects
- Audio codes are:
    - dialogue, including accent and vocabulary choice
    - sound effects
    - music
    - voice over/narration
    - use of silence
    - diegetic and non-diegetic sound
- Written codes are:
    - titles
    - captions
    - credits
    - headlines

- Mise-en-scène (to put in place).

DROP DOWN LIST - WHAT SHOULD I KNOW ABOUT IT?
- Conventions such as persuasion techniques used in documentaries. e.g.
    - interviews
    - archival footage
    - testimonials
    - emotional appeal
    - voice over/narration
    - statistics
    - authority figures
    - re-enactments/dramatisation

- Genre conventions such as:
    - iconography
    - narrative structure
    - theme
    - narrative elements

- Editing conventions such as:
    - eye-line match used to position the characters and create a consistency in screen space
    - Manipulation of time e.g., flash forward, flashback, slow motion ...
    - Manipulation of space. e.g., sound, such as siren, indicating extended space beyond the frame
    - rhythm and pace (created through sound, cinematography, and editing)

- Narrative conventions such as a traditional linear cause and effect structure.

CONTEXT

DEFINITION: refers to the background behind a fact, event or period, or the circumstances surrounding an event.

DROP DOWN LIST - WHAT SHOULD I KNOW ABOUT IT?

- Audience, context, and content are interlinked to create the text's **preferred meaning.**

- **Cultural context** is an umbrella term which includes historical, social, political, and economic contexts which surround the interpretation of an event, issue or group. Contextual elements frequently can be categorised under many headings, an event could be historical context but can also speak to the cultural context of the era.

- A text cannot be separated from its context. Context will always affect content. Discuss the **production context** (when, where and why the text was made), as well as the **reception context** (who is consuming the text and why).

- **Production context** shapes a text through:
  - contextual events
  - available technology
  - audience expectations for the era
  - agenda
  - budget
  - influences

REPRESENTATION

DEFINITION: re-present a filtered version of reality to the audience; it is not the real world, but a mediated version of the world constructed via a **value laden choice of codes.**

DROP DOWN LIST - WHAT SHOULD I KNOW ABOUT IT?

1. **Codes and conventions** – discuss how the choice of codes shapes the construction of the representation.
2. **Values** - state the values embedded in the choice of codes.
3. **Simplification** – when a representation is continually used it produces a stereotype due to the simplified visual and aural traits being used as a short cut in meaning. The narrow choice of codes leads to simplified and inaccurate representations.
4. **Selection and omission** – what is excluded, what is foregrounded? Representations privilege certain views, ages, ethnicities, genders and so on.
5. **Context** – representations are not made in a vacuum; they are created within a set of cultural and social norms.

- **Stuart Hall** claims we have a 'shared cultural map' which allows for a similar frame of reference for **encoding and decoding** to occur in an understandable manner. Hall states that representations take shape through 'language' which is any sign or symbol which can communicate meaning.

SUBCULTURE

DEFINITION: Subcultures are small groups that share the same interests, values, beliefs, and ideas.

DROP DOWN LIST - WHAT SHOULD I KNOW ABOUT IT?

- Representations of subcultures resort to stereotypical traits as a visual short cut.

- **Stereotypes** form around repeated use of generalised physical traits or behaviours which create a **short cut in meaning** for an entire group. People do not necessarily choose to be stereotyped but can easily fall into stereotypical categories due to **observable traits.**

- **Subcultures** can embrace the stereotypical traits that are attached to them. People usually (but not always) choose to be in a subculture, they choose to engage with the beliefs, norms, and values of the group. Moreover, to signal that they belong to the group, people frequently adopt a dress code and mannerisms which align with group norms thus making them susceptible to stereotyping.

- When discussing subcultures, it is important to distinguish how people **signal their belonging to the group.** Clearly investigate what identifies them by discussing aspects such as **clothing, speech patterns, behaviours, activities, and actions.** As a person usually chooses to belong to a subculture it is equally important to examine their **values and beliefs** - what do they value? How does this deviate from the norm?

- Subcultures are often discussed in terms of deviance from mainstream culture, as wanting to resist or deviate from aspects of the dominant culture.

COMMUNICATION THEORY

DEFINITION: Mass communication theories critique, explore and question the impact the mass media has on people. They investigate how and why audiences interpret and use media content.

DROP DOWN LIST - WHAT SHOULD I KNOW ABOUT IT?

Communication theories apply a model to examine how media directly or indirectly influences its mass audience. Theories range from direct effects models such as the Hypodermic Needle Theory which positions the media as all powerful and the audience as passive, through to indirect effects such as Stuart Hall's Reception Theory which considers how an active audience interprets a media text.

- Theories to consider when looking at how an audience engages with a media text:
  - Reception Theory
  - Uses and Gratifications Theory
  - Hypodermic Needle Theory
  - Reinforcement Theory
  - Agenda Setting Theory
  - Spiral of Silence
  - Diffusion of Innovation
  - Semiotic Theory
  - Two Step Flow Theory
  - Cultivation Theory

AUDIENCE

DEFINITION: The target audience or intended audience is the group of people who collectively listen to, or watch an event, performance, or production.

DROP DOWN LIST - WHAT SHOULD I KNOW ABOUT IT?

- The **primary audience** is the main **target audience.** These are the people the producer intends as the recipients of the content and message of the text.
- The main content is not directly targeted or intended for the **secondary audience**, however they will frequently engage with it due to their connection with the primary group.
- The **tertiary audience** are people on the periphery; they are outside of the direct intended circle of recipients for the content.
- A **niche audience** is a focused, small, targeted segment of the audience.
- **Mainstream** content has **wide appeal** and caters to a **mass** mainstream demographic.
- **Demographic metrics** include quantifiable elements such as the age, gender, occupation, and ethnicity of the audience.
- **Geographic** factors focus on where the audience lives, which can impact cultural understanding.
- **Psychographic** variables delve into what the audience desires by connecting with their likes, dislikes, values, beliefs, and lifestyle choices.
- Theories to consider when looking at how an audience engages with a media text:
    - Reception Theory
    - Uses and Gratifications Theory
    - Hypodermic Needle Theory
    - Reinforcement Theory
    - Agenda Setting Theory
    - Spiral of Silence
    - Diffusion of Innovation
    - Semiotic Theory
    - Two Step Flow Theory
    - Cultivation Theory

VALUES & IDEOLOGIES

DEFINITION: Values are something people believe in or aspire to. Ideologies refer to a set of beliefs or practices that enable a society to function in an organised way.

DROP DOWN LIST - WHAT SHOULD I KNOW ABOUT IT?

- Does the text promote, challenge, reinforce, confirm, endorse, or subvert the dominant ideologies?
- What values and ideologies are embedded in the **protagonist/antagonist?** Quite often the protagonist embeds values society sees as good, and the antagonist is embedded with values society sees as bad.
- What values and ideologies are revealed in the **conflict and resolution**? Does good win over evil? Does love reign supreme? What value or ideology is privileged? Whose agenda is served?
- What values are revealed by the **character's actions and appearance?** Deconstruct the **codes and conventions** used to **represent** the protagonist and antagonist. What visual and aural signifiers are used to direct the audience toward what is valued in terms of appearance and actions?
- Values and ideologies are **contextual**. What do they say about the culture of the time? **Representations matter** - what is foregrounded, what is omitted? How does this illustrate dominant values and ideologies within society at the time?
- Ideologies can be **dominant**, supported by the majority; **emerging** whereby a growing amount of people are beginning to embrace the beliefs and values; or **oppositional** whereby they are rejected outright by a vocal group.

 **NARRATIVE**

DEFINITION: The linking of cause and effect to tell a story which arises out of a specific context.

DROP DOWN LIST - WHAT SHOULD I KNOW ABOUT IT?

- **Narrative elements** - the basic elements contained in narratives are characters, setting, conflict and resolution. These elements are the scaffold upon which the story and plot are built.
- **Narrative structure** - the framework for how the story unfolds. How are the events ordered? What is the significance of the narrative sequence? How is point of view used to position the viewer?
- **Narrative theories** - create a framework for scaffolding the narrative progression of the plot. e.g., Gustav Freytag's pyramid, Claude Lévi-Strauss' binary oppositions, Tzvetan Todorov's theory of equilibrium, disequilibrium, and enigma.
- **Genre** - the audience has an expectation of the plot structure and events depending on the genre. Stephen Neale's theory of repetition and difference posits that the audience requires repetition for familiarity, however difference is required to maintain continued interest in the genre. Discuss **iconography** used to maintain familiarity.
- **Theme** is the main message which recurs throughout the narrative. A theme is also known as the moral, main idea or unifying concept within the story.
- **Point of view** - from whose point of view do we see the narrative unfold? Through selection and omission what information is relayed to the audience by this character?

 **MEDIA THEORIES**

DEFINITION: Media theories refer to any model or study which examines the impact media content has on a mass audience, or explains a concept, supported with evidence relating to mass media.

DROP DOWN LIST - WHAT SHOULD I KNOW ABOUT IT?

- **Narrative theories** create a framework for scaffolding the narrative progression of the plot. e.g.,
  - Freytag's pyramid - Gustav Freytag
  - Binary oppositions - Claude Lévi-Strauss
  - Todorov's theory - Tzvetan Todorov
- **Communication theorists** have investigated how audiences interpret and use the media they consume. Communication theories include:
  - Uses and Gratifications Theory
  - Hypodermic Needle Theory
  - Reinforcement Theory
  - Agenda Setting Theory
  - Spiral of Silence
  - Diffusion of Innovation
  - Semiotic Theory
  - Two Step Flow Theory
  - Cultivation Theory
- **Representation theory** - Stuart Hall posits that for representation to occur we need a shared conceptual map which allows members of a culture to effectively communicate. He states that language choice (visual, verbal, aural or kinetic code) is crucial to communicate meaning. How meaning is constructed about an event, issue, idea, or group occurs through a choice of codes which shape representations.
- Stephen Neale's **Genre theory** of **repetition and difference** discusses how genre conventions act as a starting point or baseline understood by both the audience and filmmaker to create and negotiate narrative possibilities. It means that the audience understands what could happen based on their **familiarity** with previous films in the canon but enjoy the challenge of the film-maker injecting **difference** to maintain audience engagement.

POINT OF VIEW

DEFINITION: Through whose eyes is the audience invited to view the action from?

DROP DOWN LIST - WHAT SHOULD I KNOW ABOUT IT?

- Point of view is a strategy used to construct the narrative. Through which character(s) perspective is the audience positioned to view the action?
- All media texts, whether fiction or non-fiction, construct a specific point of view. This construction could be to position an audience to support an idea or to represent a subject in a positive or negative way.
- Point of view can be established through the subjective use of the camera which shows the audience what the character is looking at. The audience sees only what the character sees and therefore is more likely to align with them.
- Point of view can shape audience response by raising questions regarding the conflict, characters, and resolution.
- Theme can be revealed via point of view through the values and ideologies embedded in characters and their actions.

TRENDS

DEFINITION: The direction in which something is developing.

DROP DOWN LIST - WHAT SHOULD I KNOW ABOUT IT?

- Digital technologies have changed the way media is consumed, how people connect, interact, and communicate. The digital revolution has created customised, individualised, more convenient viewing practices. A shift from linear to non-linear consumption has occurred.
- Trends in representation on our screens have seen more TV shows and movies reflecting the fabric of diversity within society.
- Trending media issues include electoral interference, data mining, the rise of disinformation, fake news, the use of bots and trolls to generate and amplify misinformation, citizen journalists using social media to convey their opinion, often blurring the lines between fact and opinion.
- The trend of having a highly curated digital feed of information which forms an echo chamber of ideas, which in turn creates a narrow world view.
- Simultaneous, multi-platform consumption of content using a few devices at once has meant that marketers can tap into an audience's desire for interactivity. Advertisers are turning to social media to target consumers and fine-tuning product placement to allow for seamless narrative progression, unhindered by traditional advertising slots.
- Technology's evolution has shaped the physical, social, and cultural landscape of society. The impact of technology on popular culture can be seen in the entertainment we consume, how we access information, how we visually represent our world, and perhaps more importantly, in how the means of telling stories and distributing information is now accessible to everyone, not just a powerful few.
- Impact of artificial intelligence.

CONTROLS, CONSTRAINTS

DEFINITION: Any factor which limits or enables media production, shaping its content through specific controls and/or constraints.

DROP DOWN LIST - WHAT SHOULD I KNOW ABOUT IT?

- Controls and constraints both enable and limit productions. They include moral, ethical, legal considerations and ownership of media assets.
- Regulatory bodies, such as the Office of Film and Literature Classification, who produce Codes of Conduct often self-regulate. Other examples include the Media, Entertainment & Arts Alliance, the Journalist Code of Ethics, the Commercial Television Industry Code of Practice, the Commercial Radio Code of Practice, the Australian Press Council, the Australian Code of Practice on Disinformation and Misinformation. These codes serve as a moral compass when making ethical decisions regarding media content.
- Legal constraints include defamation and libel. The Australian Competition & Consumer Commission, the Australian Broadcasting Corporation Act 1983, and the Special Broadcasting Service Act 1991 all serve to protect fair practice and promote Australian media interests.
- Controls and constraints may include
    ▸ production constraints such as time, budget, and personnel, technological constraints,
    ▸ audience expectations of values, ideologies, and contextual issues,
    ▸ institution and ownership, consider who owns the media asset, what is their agenda and where is revenue derived from? Does the revenue source impact on the media content?
    ▸ censorship and control.
- Australian Communications and Media Authority (ACMA) regulates Australian media by specifying rules for all content, including advertising. It advocates for Australian media by specifying a quota of Australian content that must be aired by a station each year.
- Classifications as set out by the Australian Commercial Television Code of Practice regulates the content of free-to-air television in Australia. The Australian Classification Board, has as its function to classify and censor films, video games and publications using the G, PG, M, MA15+, R and X rating system which considers coarse language, sexual content and violence when determining a target audience.

PERSUASIVE TECHNIQUES

DEFINITION: A technique deliberately employed to persuade the audience to respond to a particular argument, character or point of view.

DROP DOWN LIST - WHAT SHOULD I KNOW ABOUT IT?

- Persuasive techniques employ strategies designed to play on emotion. Consider word choice, music, choice of setting, camera work, editing pace, lighting, use of humour, deliberate choice of codes and conventions such as selection, omission, or documentary techniques.
- Documentary techniques such as:
    ○ straw man
    ○ emotional appeal
    ○ oversimplification
    ○ card stacking
    ○ scapegoating
    ○ common man
    ○ stereotyping/labelling
    ○ selection and omission
    ○ choice of authority figure, expert, witness
    ○ juxtaposition and/or binary oppositions
    ○ exposition
    ○ voice-over
    ○ choice of footage
    ○ re-enactments or dramatisation

INSTITUTIONS

DEFINITION: Media institutions refer to organisations which follow formal structural conventions (charters, acts, regulations) or informal conventions (code of ethics, norms, values) that create their culture.

DROP DOWN LIST - WHAT SHOULD I KNOW ABOUT IT?

- Commercial media is privately owned, derives its revenue through advertising or subscriptions.
- Community media is not for profit, operated mainly by volunteers voicing issues and information pertinent to that community.
- Public broadcasters are funded by the government through taxpayers providing informative public interest journalism free from commercial influences or political bias.
- Ownership of media assets matter as owners can influence the ideological landscape.
- There is a lack of diversity in media voices in Australian media due to a concentration of media asset ownership.
- Elite voices, such as Rupert Murdoch's News Corp, have the power to set the public agenda.
- Cross-media ownership laws allow media barons to penetrate the media landscape, spreading their ideological messages far and wide.
- Media diversity or having competing voices in the media landscape is crucial for a healthy democracy.
- The ABC and SBS have seen significant funding cuts over the past few years resulting in a loss of jobs and a reduced ability to cover public interest stories. The ensuing consequence is a reduction in the watchdog capabilities of our public broadcasters.
- Codes of conduct and regulatory bodies exist in Australia to regulate and guide institutions.
- Local media such as newspapers or radio losing out to social media or conglomerates reducing the local voice and content in news reporting.

GLOBALISATION

DEFINITION: is the global interconnectedness of all countries, groups, and individuals. It is the exchange of goods and ideas which allows for an integrated world.

DROP DOWN LIST - WHAT SHOULD I KNOW ABOUT IT?

- Discuss cultural imperialism, the ability of a large nation to saturate a smaller nation with its media content thereby imparting its values and ideologies.
- Media content is a product of its culture; therefore, globalisation allows for ideas to diffuse between countries.
  - Positives include exchanging and building on knowledge and skills,
  - Negatives include continuing the digital divide between those that can access media content and those who can't.
- Media conglomerates being culpable for allowing misinformation/disinformation to spread due to their lack of locally sourced operatives to assist with content moderation.
- Problems arising from global media businesses not being able to keep up with their own growth.

PREFERRED MEANING

DEFINITION: Dominant or preferred reading – the audience shares and accepts the intended meaning. The sender and receiver share similar ideological perspectives.

DROP DOWN LIST - WHAT SHOULD I KNOW ABOUT IT?

- Stuart Hall's encoding/decoding Reception Theory model posits that an audience can read a media text in three distinct ways: **dominant, negotiated, or oppositional.**
  1. Dominant or preferred reading – the audience shares and accepts the intended meaning. The sender and receiver share similar ideological perspectives.
  2. Negotiated reading – the audience understands the dominant position but doesn't necessarily subscribe to that ideology.
  3. Oppositional reading – whilst understanding the dominant meaning, the audience chooses to reject it.
- The producer encodes meaning via codes and conventions and the audience decodes meaning using the given visual and aural signifiers to arrive at a preferred, negotiated, or oppositional reading of the text.
- Hall's findings emphasised the importance of the tools available to people to assist them to deconstruct a text; specifically social or cultural capital, such as access to education and a variety of cultural discourses. He claimed that cultural, social, and geographic context shapes people in relation to race, class, gender, and age. A person's social position relative to these factors scaffolds how they will decode meaning as they will have certain codes available to them which create interpretations of meaning. The role of the audience is complex – it is not a matter of simply ingesting the content and arriving at a preferred meaning; the process of encoding and decoding is steeped in cultural, political, and social understandings which influence meaning. Moreover, the audience can mentally negotiate or actively resist the preferred meaning; although factors such as race, class, age, or gender shape meaning, they do not permanently fix it in place.

SELECTION, OMISSION

DEFINITION: What content is deliberately included and what omitted?

DROP DOWN LIST - WHAT SHOULD I KNOW ABOUT IT?

- Through selection and omission what information is relayed to the audience?
- What codes and conventions have media produces selected to represent people, ideas, issues, or places? What has been omitted?
- Whose agenda is served by selection of content or omission of content?
- What is privileged or foregrounded? What values are embedded in the foregrounding of specific content?
- Does selection and/or omission change the meaning of content for the viewer?

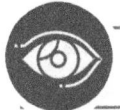
MEDIA INFLUENCE

DEFINITION: Media influence is tethered to how much media a person consumes, what content they engage with, and the medium they use to extract the information or entertainment from.

DROP DOWN LIST - WHAT SHOULD I KNOW ABOUT IT?

- Media representations **influence** the construction and circulation of meaning. The media can shape representations of gender, sexual orientation, race, religion, ethnicity, and age.
- Antonio Gramsci argued that cultural institutions such as the media spread selected information and therefore wield **ideological influence.** The role of the media in selecting or omitting information is crucial in shaping how we view ourselves and others.
- **Media influence** can be scaffolded using communication theories such as the Two-Step Flow Theory, the Reinforcement Theory, the Agenda Setting Theory, the Uses and Gratification Theory, the Spiral of Silence, and the Cultivation Theory.
- Media techniques employed to influence an audience:
  - selected codes and conventions to shape the preferred meaning and influence the audience.
  - point of view
  - discourse
  - embedding values and ideologies
  - manipulating emotions via persuasive techniques.

THEME

DEFINITION: A **theme** is the main message which recurs throughout the narrative.

DROP DOWN LIST - WHAT SHOULD I KNOW ABOUT IT?

- How is the **theme** communicated to the audience? What codes and conventions have been employed to construct **characters** and in doing so represent theme? Deconstruct the actions, behaviours, values, dialogue, and intentions of the main characters.
- Does the **setting** allow for the characters to reveal or reinforce the theme?
- How does the **conflict** and **resolution** convey the theme?
- How do the chosen codes and conventions communicate the theme?
- What values and ideologies are embedded in the theme?

Year 12 drop-down lists of essential content

The drop-down lists of essential content for Year 11 and Year 12 have some similarities and some differences due to the different contexts studied. Refer to the relevant year group to enhance your study.

Studying for an in-class assessment or exam means that you should have a substantial amount of knowledge about the examinable essential content terms found in the syllabus. When you read any question, you should have an 'essential content drop-down list' of information regarding what you could potentially write about. For example, if a question contains the term NARRATIVE, what are some points that could be discussed? A sound suggestion is to learn the drop-down list of essential content associated with each term.

For example, NARRATIVE possible discussions points are:

- Narrative **structure**: how are the events ordered — linear cause and effect, non-linear, elliptical, episodic? Consider manipulation of time and space.
- Narrative **theory** such as:
    - Todorov's equilibrium, disequilibrium, return to equilibrium
    - Claude Levi Strauss' binary oppositions
    - Syd Field
    - Freytag's Pyramid
- Narrative **elements**
    - characters
    - setting
    - conflict
    - resolution
- **Point of view** - from whose point of view do we see the narrative unfold?
- **Genre** expectations, iconography.

Should you write about all these points? **Absolutely not**. Your job is to deconstruct the question and apply the most applicable aspect of the essential content. The point of learning the 'drop-down list' is to give you concrete content to draw from rather than blankly staring at a question and not knowing what you could potentially write about.

 # CODES

 # CONVENTIONS

DEFINITION: Codes are used to construct meaning within a narrative. A director will manipulate and choose specific codes to create a preferred meaning for an intended audience.

DEFINITION: accepted ways of using film techniques to construct meaning.

DROP DOWN LIST - WHAT SHOULD I KNOW ABOUT IT?
- Symbolic codes are:
  - costume
  - objects
  - setting
  - colour
  - body language, including facial expressions
- Technical codes are:
  - lighting
  - shot size, framing
  - camera angle, movement
  - shutter speed, aperture, lens choice
  - compositional devices such as leading lines, rule of thirds, juxtaposition, contrast, positioning
  - special effects
  - editing choices - graphic, spatial, temporal, or rhythmic
- Audio codes are:
  - dialogue
  - sound effects
  - music
  - use of silence
  - voice over/narration
  - consideration of rhythm, volume, pace, and pitch
- Written codes are:
  - titles
  - captions
  - credits
  - typography
  - headlines
  - speech bubbles
- mise-en-scène

DROP DOWN LIST - WHAT SHOULD I KNOW ABOUT IT?
- Manipulation of time e.g., flash forward, flashback, slow motion, real time ...
- Manipulation of space
- Conventions such as persuasion techniques used in documentaries:
  - interviews
  - archival footage
  - testimonials
  - emotional appeal
  - voice over/narration
  - statistics
  - authority figures
  - re-enactments/dramatisation
  - juxtaposition
- Film movement conventions such as:
  - French New Wave
  - Noir & Neo-Noir
  - Surrealism
  - German Expressionism
  - Hollywood (Classical & New)
- Editing - used to establish screen space and narrative time, leading the viewer to understand what is important within the narrative. Conventions include:
  - Ideational montage, narrative montage
  - continuity editing: seamless, invisible, screen direction flows, eye-line match is used to position the characters and create a consistency in screen space allowing for suspension of disbelief
  - creation of point of view
  - manipulation of time and space
  - rhythm and pace, created through sound, cinematography, and editing
- Selection (what is foregrounded to highlight the preferred meaning) and omission (what is ignored)
- Genre conventions
- Narrative conventions

REPRESENTATION	NARRATIVE
DEFINITION: in media, texts re-present a filtered version of reality to the audience; it is not the real world but a mediated version of the world.	**DEFINITION:** is the linking of cause and effect to tell a story which arises out of a specific context.

DROP DOWN LIST - WHAT SHOULD I KNOW ABOUT IT?

Representations are created through:
- Selection processes – codes are chosen to represent the group.
- The choice of codes is value laden.
- Representations reflect their cultural context.
- Because they appear to be real, media representation shapes our perceptions of people, events, and issues.
- Representations occur of issues, events, ideas, individuals, social groupings, and institutions.
- Consider the power of the media to represent an issue through selection, omission, choice of codes and conventions, and values embedded.
- Stereotypes are recurring representations, when used often enough they can become naturalised.
- Stereotypes, by their nature, choose a few symbols to represent the whole, this simplification leads to inaccuracy.
- A stereotype is a recurring representation that reduces something complex to something simple. It is an oversimplified representation of a group of people.
- Problems associated with stereotyping:
    - Only represent a single viewpoint about a group of people.
    - Oversimplification leads to inaccuracy.
    - The stereotype is repeated so often it becomes accepted as reality and is therefore naturalised making it very difficult to change attitudes towards the group.
- Consider representation of an issue or event. How has the issue been constructed?
    - codes and conventions
    - discourse
    - values and ideologies embedded in characters, their actions, and language used
    - intended audience
    - selection and omission

DROP DOWN LIST - WHAT SHOULD I KNOW ABOUT IT?

- **Narrative structure** - how are the events ordered? Linear cause and effect, non-linear, elliptical, episodic? Consider manipulation of time and space.

- **Narrative theories** such as:
    - Todorov's equilibrium, disequilibrium, return to equilibrium
    - Claude Levi-Strauss' binary oppositions
    - Syd Field
    - Freytag's Pyramid

- **Narrative elements**:
    - characters
    - setting
    - conflict
    - resolution

- **Point of view** - from whose point of view do we see the narrative unfold? How is point of view used to position the viewer? Through selection and omission what information is relayed to the audience by the character?

- **Genre** expectations including iconography, and Stephen Neale's theory of repetition and difference.

- **Theme** is the main message which recurs throughout the narrative. A theme is also known as the moral, main idea or unifying concept within the story. How does the choice of codes, conventions and narrative elements support the theme?

AUDIENCE

DEFINITION: Audiences are complex groups of people with histories, experiences, attitudes, and values which they bring to their consumption of media texts.

DROP DOWN LIST - WHAT SHOULD I KNOW ABOUT IT?
- intended audience
- niche audience vs. mainstream
- subcultural
- audience reading/positioning
- audience theories:
  - Reception Theory - Stuart Hall -encoding/decoding
  - Uses and Gratifications
  - Hypodermic Needle
  - Reinforcement Theory
  - Agenda Setting Function

SUBCULTURE

DEFINITION: a smaller group co-existing within the mainstream culture, but having values, ideologies and beliefs which vary from the dominant group whilst unifying the subcultural group.

DROP DOWN LIST - WHAT SHOULD I KNOW ABOUT IT?
- How does a person signal their membership to a subculture? Consider aspects such as fashion, language, vocabulary, music, beliefs, and views such as religion or politics.
- Codes of construction - what codes (symbolic, audio etc) signal that a person belongs to a particular subculture?
- What value judgement is embedded in the choice of codes used to represent the subculture?
- Consider how auteur figures use personal expression to target subcultures.
- What characteristics such as interests, tastes, wants and preferences are communicated by a niche audience?

 **VALUES & IDEOLOGIES**

 **CONTEXT**

DEFINITION: Values are something people believe in or aspire to. Ideologies refer to a set of beliefs or practices that enable a society to function in an organised way.

DEFINITION: Context deals with the society of the text including the time and place, values, and attitudes and how the culture impacts on behaviour and opportunities.

DROP DOWN LIST - WHAT SHOULD I KNOW ABOUT IT?
- Does the text promote, challenge, reinforce, confirm, endorse, or subvert the dominant ideologies?
- What values are embedded in the text? Consider the actions of the protagonist and antagonist, and their appearance and dialogue. What characters do, say, and look like signal value systems.
- Film and TV have a language of their own, within which values are suggested, attitudes reinforced, and statements conveyed about society, family, and relationships.

DROP DOWN LIST - WHAT SHOULD I KNOW ABOUT IT?
- A text cannot be separated from its context. Context will always affect content. When analysing a media text, it is important to research the production context (when, where and why the text was made), as well as the reception context (who is consuming the text and why).
- Consider the political, social, cultural, and historical context surrounding the text.
- What was the intent of the production at the time it was made? Does the present day reception context alter the meaning of the text?

 **TRENDS**

DEFINITION: - a general direction in which something is developing or changing.

DROP DOWN LIST - WHAT SHOULD I KNOW ABOUT IT?
- Consider social or political trends e.g., trend of environmental awareness or the trend of liberalisation of gender values.
- Consider films which actively challenging the parameters and established trends of cinema through narrative form and visual aesthetic.
- Trends in the way audiences engage with and interpret media work (think audience theory).
- How changing trends affect media use e.g., changing audience trends and how this has involved 'borrowing' from fiction and popular culture, particularly narrative techniques, structures, and characterisation in texts such as documentaries.
- Trends in narrative construction, genres, music, and special effects.
- Trends in the perception and representation of gender roles.
- Trends in how technology shapes interactions, habits, behaviours, and responses.

 **AESTHETICS**

DEFINITION: Is the study of what makes a film artistic, visually and aurally appealing, and what gives it an edge. It is concerned with the style and form of film, and the film maker's creative intention.

DROP DOWN LIST - WHAT SHOULD I KNOW ABOUT IT?
- Innovative visual aesthetic. Consider aspects such as:
  - mise-en-scène, colour palette, technical codes such as camera movement, framing, editing details such as pace and rhythm, use of diegetic and non-diegetic sounds.
- Manipulation of narrative structure
- Character subjectivity
- Open-ended narrative
- Political and social comment
- Manipulation of time and space
- Deviation from realism
- Experimentation with rhythm, pace, and continuity editing
- Manipulation of the medium
- Auteur, personal expression
- Artistic and cultural benefits

INSTITUTIONS

DEFINITION: Media institutions refer to organisations who follow structural conventions which can be formal (charters, acts, regulations) or informal (code of ethics, norms, values) which create their culture.

DROP DOWN LIST - WHAT SHOULD I KNOW ABOUT IT?
- Mainstream media institutions need to appeal to a mass audience, therefore, to remain economically viable their film content needs to consider the dominant values and ideologies within society.
- Large media institutions mean bigger budgets and more pressure to recoup cost by attracting a large audience, therefore narratives can often conform to formulaic genre expectations which are known to work.
- Consider the effect of targeting audience and how narrative content must be suitable for the classification system associated with the intended audience.
- Ownership - who funded the film? Is an agenda attached? Are the values and ideologies of the owner represented in the content?
- Mergers and acquisitions - consider the sharing or removal of content for financial or political purposes. e.g., Disney/Fox (acquisition) and Warners/Discovery (merger).

INDEPENDENTS

DEFINITION: Film makers working outside of large institutions such as Hollywood studios are known as independent film makers.

DROP DOWN LIST - WHAT SHOULD I KNOW ABOUT IT?
- Alternative: films and videos that provide an alternative to commercial media or to conventional topics and forms, dealing with subjects, points-of-view and formal elements not found in the mainstream.
- Independent: work that is made outside of the Hollywood system. Though most experimental film and video falls into this category, it generally refers to non-Hollywood feature and documentary films.
- Experimental: the maker experiments with the medium, the production process, or the structure of the work, without necessarily knowing what the outcome will be.
- Independent film makers stand out from mainstream media by having the freedom to critique, push boundaries and comment on social or political issues without fear of substantial economic considerations.
- Independent film makers have more creative control but fewer resources. Larger institutions have the infrastructure in place to make block buster films. Whereas independent film makers must be more innovative and focused on their intent.
- How is the film funded? Does the source of funding impact on its independence?
- Independent media offers differing points of view and provides alternate content to the mainstream thus benefiting all members of the culture, not just the dominant group.
- Exhibition - content appears at film festivals.
- More autonomy with regards to content due to less commercial pressure for economic gains.

AUTEUR THEORY

DEFINITION: Auteur: someone who shows a signature style across a body of work. Personal expression: how a film maker encodes meaning through the choice of specific codes, conventions and techniques.

DROP DOWN LIST - WHAT SHOULD I KNOW ABOUT IT?

- What is the auteur's signature style? Give specific examples of codes, conventions and techniques used.
- Does the style reference conventions from film movements?
- Can you relate Andrew Sarris' privileging of the director to clear evidence in your text? Sarris posited that the following three elements, when used consistently and in unison, define a director as an auteur.
  1. The outer circle as technique (technical quality - give examples from your text).
  2. The middle circle as personal style (choice of codes and conventions - give examples from your text).
  3. The inner circle as interior meaning (relate to theme and emotion - give examples from your text).
- Pauline Kael: responded to Sarris in her 1963 essay *Circles and Squares* where she critically questioned the auteur theory by arguing that:
1. **Technical competence** is based on the judgement of the audience and critic.
2. Why should a director be congratulated for having a **distinctive style**, particularly when that style is simply different?
3. Kael questions why substance in films is ignored, and stylistic consistency praised.
- An auteur can be a director, screenwriter, producer, cinematographer, editor, music composer, costume designer, actor, production designer, or even a studio.
- Consider film marketing in relation to the director. What is the audiences' expectation of the style, inclusion of themes, collaboration with actors and techniques of the director?
- Auteur branding, particularly trading on the name of the director, cultivates a fan base and creates recognition which assists with marketing.

PRODUCTION CONTEXT

DEFINITION: Where, when, and by whom a media production is made, shapes its content.

DROP DOWN LIST - WHAT SHOULD I KNOW ABOUT IT?

- How media texts are produced, distributed, circulated, and exhibited?
- Regulation in the media - consider the film classification board.
- Propaganda and agenda setting.
- Censorship.
- Formal and informal censorship that impacts media content.
- Production context includes aspects such as:
  - Context - historical events, values and attitudes present in a particular era, popular culture trends which impact on content of media work.
  - Controls and constraints - legal and ethical considerations, classification boards and regulatory bodies and codes of conduct.
  - Technological and production factors - time, budget, cast and crew and audience expectation of genre or auteur.
  - Institutional factors - what is the main purpose of production company, commercial or non-commercial? Where is revenue derived from? Consider advertising, ticket sales, merchandise. Who owns the production company? Do they have a particular agenda to push? Who is the intended audience?

DOCUMENTARY

DEFINITION: The documentary form, as a non-fiction text is associated with realism, with its aim being to convey information about a social or political message.

DROP DOWN LIST - WHAT SHOULD I KNOW ABOUT IT?

- How do the chosen conventions, codes and techniques privilege the filmmaker's point of view?
- State the documentary **convention** and its effect
  - voice over
  - testimonials and interviews
  - archival footage
  - re-enactments/ dramatisation
  - juxtaposition
  - exposition
  - authority figures
  - statistics
  - selection, omission, emphasis
- **Persuasion techniques**:
  - bandwagon
  - assertion
  - card stacking
  - glittering generalities
  - name calling
  - oversimplification
  - stereotyping
  - common man
- **Selection and omission** can reveal the point of view of the film maker. From whose eyes do we see the story unfold?
- **A documentary is a construction**, crafted from a choice of codes, conventions, and techniques to create a preferred meaning.
  - choice of **audio code** (music, voice over, discourse ...)
  - choice of **visual information** such as graphics, archival footage, visual effects
  - **editing**, particularly ordering of events, pace and duration
  - **technical codes** such as lighting, framing and angles
  - how do written codes anchor meaning?
  - what **symbolic codes** have been chosen to construct meaning? Consider locations, objects, clothing of the presenter and so on.
- **Agenda** - what is the film maker's agenda and how does it drive the point of view.
- **Bill Nichols** documentary modes:
  - poetic, observational, expository, participatory, performative, reflexive.

PROPAGANDA

DEFINITION: To propagate or spread ideas or information in a deliberate manner designed to influence other's beliefs, attitudes and behaviours about a cause, institution, or person.

DROP DOWN LIST - WHAT SHOULD I KNOW ABOUT IT?

- State the idea or message being spread.
- Discuss the codes used to position the audience to decode the preferred meaning.
- Discuss the values and ideologies embedded.
- Discuss the context - why is this message being spread?
- Discuss the agenda behind the spreading of the information.

- Propaganda can be used to convey an ideology, often by employing misinformation or disinformation to propel its agenda. Propaganda flourishes when people do not authenticate or critically evaluate sources of information. It is important to triangulate information by referring to multiple sources from differing perspectives to challenge pre-existing beliefs.

Sample drop-down list
Applied to The Fresh Prince of Bel-Air

NARRATIVE CONVENTIONS

DROP DOWN LIST
- **Narrative elements** - characters, setting, conflict, resolution.
- **Narrative structure** - in relation to TV: stable state, disruption, inject novelty, return to stable state.
- **Narrative theory** - Todorov, Lévi-Strauss.
- **Narrative story elements** - point of view, cause and effect, relationship of opening sequence to resolution.

Note that the drop-down list is short and sweet to assist with recall in a timed assessment. Additionally, not all elements from the drop-down list must be used when answering a question.

1. **Narrative elements** form the backbone of plot construction. The use of characters, setting, conflict and resolution shape any genre. In the case of *Fresh Prince of Bel-Air* (1990), the genre is a situation comedy, constructed from iconic narrative elements.
   → Expand by giving **specificity of examples** for each of the narrative elements.

2. **The form of television** can be seen affecting its content. **Todorov's narrative theory** highlights how **segmentation** and structural aspects of TV are unique to the medium. *The Fresh Prince of Bel-Air's* opening, rather than convey basic cast information, is a complete back-story in itself. The title sequence employs vibrant colours, slap stick comedy, rap music, artistic graffiti and a cartoon feel to succinctly convey the protagonist, Will Smith's back story. Initially the audience is introduced to Will as he enjoys his everyday life in **equilibrium.** We see him chillin' out maxin', relaxin' and playing basketball with his neighbourhood friends. **Disequilibrium** occurs when Will gets into 'one little fight' and his mother tells him he is "movin' with your aunt and uncle in Bel-Air" The infectious rap music creates a sense of **immediacy,** the **repetition** of the opening sequence in every episode allows for viewer **familiarity. Segmentation chunks** the narrative into pieces, consisting of the opening sequence which follows Todorov's narrative theory, only bringing the story to a **new equilibrium** at the conclusion of the episode when the audience sees Will playing Für Elise on the piano, signalling to his uncle that he is not totally wrapped up in the urban rap ghetto world but has the capacity to assimilate into the Banks' upper class world.

3. **Conflict** occurs due to pairs of opposed forces colluding; thus, **Levi Strauss' structuralist binary oppositions** have been employed to create conflict and determine ideological messages. Specifically, this can be seen in the binary opposites below:
   - rich vs. poor
   - Will's street 'ghetto' dress sense vs. the conservative dress of the Banks' family
   - safety vs. violence/danger
   - tough neighbourhood of West Philadelphia vs. Bel-Air
   - rap/beat box music vs classical music
   - street language vs. conservative language
   - low income vs wealthy

   Language and dress form a class divide issue as Phil critiques Will's dress sense and language choice.
   → Expand by giving **specificity of examples** for a few of the binary oppositions and explaining the underlying ideological message.

Sample drop-down list
Applied to The Fresh Prince of Bel-Air

VALUES & IDEOLOGIES

DROP DOWN LIST
- **Values and ideologies embedded in the protagonist/antagonist.** The protagonist embeds values society sees as good; the antagonist is embedded with values society sees as bad.
- **Values and ideologies revealed in the conflict and resolution.** Does good win over evil, does love reign supreme …?
- **Values and ideologies revealed in the characters' actions and appearance.** Are kind actions privileged? What style or look is privileged?

Note textual examples have been provided in green or a statement has been supplied where specificity of examples is required in order to exemplify the essential content for the examiner.

1. Will is encoded via symbolic, technical, and audio codes which highlight his confident, rebellious, independent, and caring personality.
→ Expand by giving **specificity of examples** for each of the codes.

1. **Value of respect** - portrayal of Banks family as hard working, educated, socially accomplished. Phil Banks states, 'We promised your mother that you are here to work hard, straighten out and learn some good old American values.' Links to theme of politics of respectability through education, tradition, and hard work.
→ Dinner party scene reveals **value of individuality** Expand by giving **specificity of examples** explaining how Will acts and dresses. His confidence in himself is portrayed through his body language and unfazed nature thus highlighting the **value of individuality** and being comfortable in one's own look.

2. Will's character is embedded with the **values of kindness and friendliness.** Firstly, when Will arrives at the Banks' household he hugs the butler, mistaking him for his Uncle Phil. Secondly, when Will first meets his cousin Ashley, he leans down to kiss her hand, saying "My little Scottish cousin" in reference to her tartan school skirt. Later Will spends time with his younger cousin when she tells him that she didn't get into her school choir because her teacher thought her to be tone deaf. Will comforts and distracts Ashley by teaching her how to rap. The **kindness Will embodies** is used to engage and connect with the mainstream 13+ audience as this value crosses gender and cultural boundaries.

3. **Humour is a value** that connects to an audience, blurring class, gender, and race boundaries. Will's character is extremely humorous, he approaches situations in a light-hearted manner.
→ Expand by giving **specificity of examples** explaining how Will is humorous. Thus, the **value of humour** is used as a vehicle to connect with the show's 13+ mainstream audience.

4. Discuss **ideologies of patriarchy, the familial ideology, materialism,** and **environmentalism.**
→ Expand by giving **specificity of examples** explaining how each ideology circulates dominant ideas via the narrative.

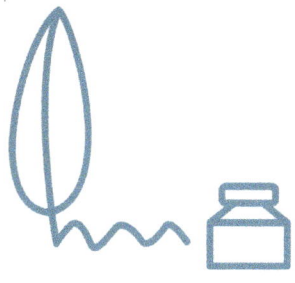

Chapter Eight

Media theories summary

- Communication/audience theories
- Narrative theories
- Representation theory
- Auteur theory
- Identity theory - David Gauntlett
- Genre theory - Stephen Neale

Media Theories Summary

Summary of media theories

Media theories refer to any model or study which examines the impact media content has on a mass audience or explains a concept, supported with evidence relating to mass media production.

You may be asked to answer assessment questions on media theories. This chapter covers some, but not all, of the theories you may choose to refer to:
- Communication/audience theories
- Narrative theories
- Representation theory
- Auteur theory
- Genre theory
- Identity theory

The above mentioned theories are explained in detail in the books *Understanding and Applying Media Theory* for Year 11 and, the second book *Understanding and Applying Media Theory* for Year 12. Moreover, in the books the theories are applied to films, advertisements, and television episodes to showcase how you can incorporate academic theories into your assessments.

Note that some of the gendered terms associated with the theories have been kept as they reflect their context. They are in no way meant to offend or exclude. Gendered terms signal the historical and cultural context of the theorists.

Summary of communication theories

COMMUNICATION THEORY DEFINED

Communication theories apply a model to examine how media directly or indirectly influences its mass audience. Theories range from direct effects models such as the Hypodermic Needle Theory which positions the media as all powerful and the audience as passive, through to indirect effects such as Stuart Hall's Reception Theory which considers how an active audience interprets a media text.

Communication theorists investigate how audiences interpret and use the media they consume. When discussing audience effects, it is possible to refer to any number of theorists summarised in the following pages. Choose a theorist who best supports the essential content required to deconstruct your text.

Semiotic Theory

The study of signs and symbols, what they signify and how they convey meaning. Texts are encoded by producers and decoded by the audience.

1900s — Ferdinand de Saussure

Hypodermic Needle

Media content is injected directly into an audience's consciousness without the individual filtering or mediating the message in any way.

1920-30s — Frankfurt School & Payne Fund

Two Step Flow

Information is gathered by an opinion leader who filters it and then passes it on to family, peers, and friends.

1948 — Paul Lazarsfeld

Reinforcement Theory

Promotes the idea that audiences would be more likely to accept and support an idea if it already aligns with their pre-existing values and ideas.

1960 — Joseph Klapper

Summary of communication theories

Diffusion of Innovation

Examines how and why an innovation such as a new idea, product, behaviour and so on spreads over time and space in a predictable manner.

1962 — Everett Rogers

Agenda Setting Theory

The media can't tell the audience what to think, but they can tell them what to think about.

1972 — McCombs and Shaw

Reception Theory

How an audience is positioned to view a text: dominant, negotiated, or oppositional reading.

1973 — Stuart Hall

Spiral of Silence

Examines why people stay silent on issues of importance when they judge that their view differs from the majority.

1974 — Elisabeth Noelle-Neumann

Cultivation Theory

Looks at the effect of habitual, cumulative exposure of television and how this impacted people's beliefs and vision of their social reality.

1970s-80s — Gerbner and Gross

Uses & Gratifications

Looks at what people do with the media, rather than what the media does to people. Media is used to gratify social and psychological desires.

1970s-80s — Blumler, Katz, McQuail, Lull

Summary of narrative theories

 Gustav Freytag

... a German playwright who diagrammed a method of mapping story progression in the shape of a pyramid which follows the course of a five act play.

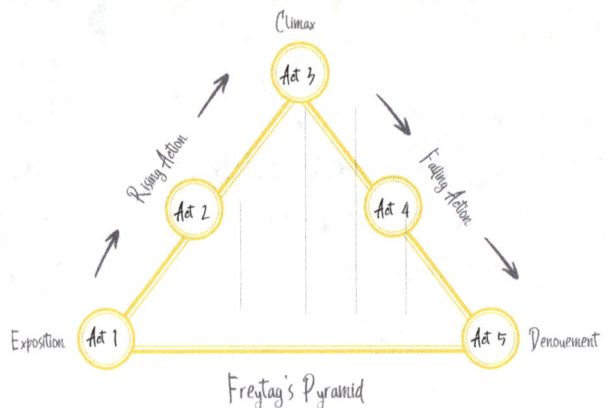

Gustav Freytag's pyramid contains five sections:

1. Exposition
2. Rising action
3. Climax
4. Falling action
5. Denouement

Tzvetan Todorov

... a Bulgarian-French literary critic and author, proposed a narrative theory which states that all stories follow a similar pattern and use five clear stages.

1. Equilibrium - the narrative begins in balance.
2. Disruption - an event occurs which disrupts the balance and harmony.
3. Recognition - a recognition that order has been broken. Disequilibrium occurs.
4. Repair - tension exists as an attempt is made to repair the damage.
5. Reinstatement - conflicts are resolved, normality restored, and equilibrium is reinstated.

Summary of narrative theories

Vladimir Propp

... a Russian scholar who analysed over one hundred Russian folk tales and saw commonalities in narrative structures.

He identified eight character roles that he attributed narrative functions to:

1. Hero - a main character who overcomes obstacles in order to achieve a goal.
2. Villain - a character who attempts to foil the hero.
3. Dispatcher - a character who sends the hero on his/her way as they attempt to achieve a set goal or task.
4. Donor - a character who provides the hero with an essential, sometimes magical object.
5. Princess - a character who acts as a reward for the hero achieving his/her goal. It could be a love interest, or it could be someone who delivers peace, truth, or justice.
6. Helper - a character who helps the hero achieve his/her goal.
7. False hero - a character who acts like the hero but is deceptive and will often try to steal the reward or essential object away from the hero.
8. Father - a character who rewards the hero and can assist in guarding the magical object.

Syd Field

... American screenwriter, in his 1979 book *Screenplay: The Foundations of Screen Writing* proposed the "three act structure" in relation to the narrative construction of films.

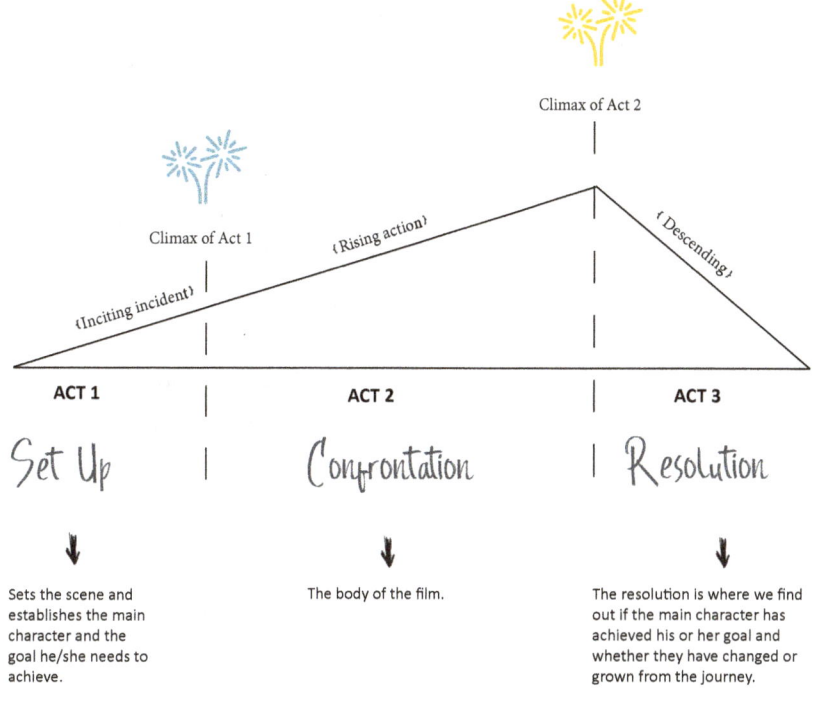

Set Up — Sets the scene and establishes the main character and the goal he/she needs to achieve.

Confrontation — The body of the film.

Resolution — The resolution is where we find out if the main character has achieved his or her goal and whether they have changed or grown from the journey.

Summary of narrative theories

Claude Lévi-Strauss
*... proposed that conflict occurs due to **pairs of opposed forces colliding***

Lévi-Strauss, a 20th century French structural anthropologist, suggested the idea that binary oppositions are used in narratives to fuel audience engagement by creating contrasting characters and ideas. Some examples include:

- Country vs. city
- Truth vs. lies
- Good vs. evil
- Human vs. supernatural
- Rational vs. emotional
- Young vs. old
- Strong vs. weak
- Knowledge vs. ignorance
- Protagonist vs. antagonist
- Man vs. nature
- Domestic vs. foreign or alien
- Tradition vs. change

Binary oppositions are **not neutral**, they are value laden, privileging one element over another.

Joseph Campbell
... the hero's journey details the path the protagonist must take to overcome obstacles and achieve his or her goal.

Joseph Campbell's 1949 plot template refers to the structure of stories which follow the narrative progression of an unwitting hero who finds himself on a journey, learns something about himself at a decisive moment in the plot, puts this new-found knowledge to use, triumphs over adversity, then returns home transformed by his adventure. Chris Vogler's adaptation of Joseph Campbell's hero's journey can be found in his book 'The Writer's Journey: Mythic Structure for Writers' which frames Campbell's narrative structure into the following:

1. The Ordinary World
2. The Call to Adventure
3. Refusal of the Call
4. Meeting the Mentor
5. Crossing the First Threshold
6. Tests, Allies, Enemies
7. Approach to the Inmost Cave
8. The Ordeal
9. Reward
10. The Road Back
12. Return with the Elixir

Summary of narrative theories

 **Roland Barthes** ... a French literary and social critic, suggested that stories contain five main narrative codes which the audience uses to try and make sense of the plot.

1. Enigma code - these are little puzzles or clues which the audience combines to try and decipher the narrative.
2. Action code - this code adds suspense and sequential action.
3. Semantic code - refers to elements within the text which hold a connotative function.
4. Symbolic code - used to enhance character development and create tension. Similar to the semantic code however it deals more with binary oppositions.
5. Referential code - refers to the audience's prior contextual knowledge of elements in the narrative which may refer to historical, political, cultural, and social events.

As with all theories, you need to apply the one that suits the question and your content. Do not attempt to apply all theories to your media text when answering a question. It is better to show depth of understanding by giving specific textual examples and explaining how the theory supports your thesis rather than superficially covering numerous theories without evidence or support.

Media and English Literacy ©2019

Summary of representation theory

Professor Stuart Hall, a ground-breaking British cultural studies theorist examined the relationship between culture and power. He explored the importance of people having 'shared cultural maps' expressed through language (visual, aural, and kinetic) and how this shaped their view of the world through **representations.**

For society to function effectively we need to have 'shared cultural maps' or shared ways of encoding and decoding information to understand each other and the world around us. Imagine how different it would be if we all decoded the connotations of colours differently, or if we placed our own meaning onto signs or words. Communication would be slow and complicated. All signs and symbols, or 'language systems' evolve, shift, and change to reflect their context. Shared cultural maps are not static, they evolve constantly, using **signs and symbols** to communicate cultural markers of the era.

Stuart Hall's study of **representation** is useful to apply to deconstructing media texts. Sign systems, such as language and image choice, shape representations. How something is described attributes positive or negative connotations to the representation thus making a value judgement about the group, issue or concept being represented. As **representations** are constructed via a choice of codes, meaning is contestable. However, media texts frequently employ stereotypes to 'fix' meaning, thereby laying the foundation for the **representation** to create a preferred reading.

Making meaning of a media text requires that the viewer deconstruct or interpret the given signs in a similar way to that which was intended by the producer of the text; therefore having a **'shared cultural map'** assists the viewer to understand the meaning constructed. **Stuart Hall** describes meaning as being created by a given code. The producer and viewer share a conceptual map which gives them access to deconstruct the shared codes, thus a **'system of representation'** is created through the codes in order to effectively communicate meaning.

Shared cultural maps allow for understandable **encoding and decoding** to occur. For these shared cultural maps to grow a clear frame of reference needs to be built between participants in a culture. **Stuart Hall** posits that 'language' or sign systems are the backbone for creating clear communication. **Representations take shape through 'language' or sign systems.**

Stuart Hall links the construction and use of **representations to power.** Attempting to fix meaning to signs and symbols reveals a bias or agenda. Consider the people who have historically owned and made media texts - for decades the vast majority were male, white and heterosexual. Their view of the world permeated media content. Representations of gender, sexuality, race and so on were narrow, reflecting the ideology of the producer which attempted to "fix" meaning to aspects of society such as race and gender roles. When these representations are shown repeatedly, they form stereotypical understandings of the world. Stuart Hall argues that representations matter as they have the power to control the construction and circulation of meaning. Consider how representation of sexual orientation, gender roles and race has changed slowly over the last decade to include more diversity thus beginning to circulate emerging values and ideologies which challenge historical understanding.

Summary of representation theory

1. SHARED CULTURAL MAP

Stuart Hall claims we have a 'shared cultural map' which allows for a similar frame of reference for encoding and decoding to occur in an understandable manner.

2. CONCEPTS

For this map to take shape we need to classify and categorise concepts, ideas, issues, groups and so on, in a similar fashion.

3. REPRESENTATION, CULTURE AND LANGUAGE

Representation starts to take shape through language. Stuart Hall suggests that without language (sign systems), meaning could not be exchanged. A representation portrays a slice of the truth, it selects a slice of reality from a choice of specific codes and conventions and shapes it, often reinforcing stereotypical traits. Frequently representations serve an agenda which can be political in nature, cultural or gendered. Representations are linked to power. It is important to question who has the power to progress representations and who has the power to silence particular representations. **Representations are not neutral; they reflect the agenda of those with power.**

1 CULTURE
Consists of a shared conceptual map which allows members of a culture to effectively communicate.

2 LANGUAGE
Stuart Hall uses the term to describe any visual, verbal, aural or kinetic code used to communicate meaning.

3 REPRESENTATION
How meaning is constructed about an event, issue, idea, or group through the choice of codes.

- **Representations** matter as they circulate values and ideologies. Often a person's only connection with a group, issue or person is through the media they consume. Their understanding is a constructed re-presentation of reality, one that comes with the agenda of the producer attached. Consider how *The Guardian* newspaper represents Donald Trump vs. *The Australian* newspaper, their representation of the man couldn't be more different, representing their differing political agendas.
- **Representations** re-present a filtered version of reality to the audience; it is not the real world, but a mediated version of the world constructed via a **value laden choice of codes.** How a person, event, place, institution, group, or issue is represented matters as meaning is created and circulated via the repeated use of words and images used to construct them.
- **Stuart Hall's Representation Theory** argues that the media is a crucial site in making and disseminating meaning. He states that the media manufactures representations by repeatedly using either positive or negative codes to portray a person, group or issue which aligns with their agenda, thus influencing audience understanding of their world.

Summary of auteur theory

An auteur is someone whose films show a signature style, technically and thematically across a body of work. An auteur can be a director, screenwriter, producer, cinematographer, editor, music composer, costume designer, actor, production designer, or even a studio. The defining characteristic is that their filmography shows a clear and recognisable stylistic or thematic signature.

The auteur theory is no longer framed around the director as the sole creative contributor to a film, rather, the collaborative nature is acknowledged and celebrated.

Brief History

1954 — **François Truffaut**, writing for the film journal *Cahier du Cinema*, wrote an essay entitled "Une certaine tendance du cinéma Français" with the central thesis being a move away from defining the director as a person who simply stages the scene, to reclassifying the director as an auteur, or author, someone who takes the creative lead in the creation of the film.

1962 — **Andrew Sarris,** an American film critic who had spent time in France and was acquainted with the critics of the *Cahier du Cinema* wrote a seminal essay, "Notes on the Auteur Theory" which privileged the primacy of the director, highlighting his authorial control to an American audience. This notion had been circulating in France and Europe since Truffaut's 1954 essay however Sarris pushed the idea to the foreground with American film critics and audiences. The intent of Sarris' essay was to highlight the value of Hollywood films as being a serious contributor to the Arts and to make people aware of the extent of creative input required by a director for a film to achieve success, as previously the actors, the story and the genre were prefaced over the director.

Sarris posited that the following three elements, when used consistently and in unison, define a director as an auteur. The auteur theory can be visualised as three concentric circles:
1. The outer circle as technique,
2. The middle circle as personal style,
3. The inner circle as interior meaning.

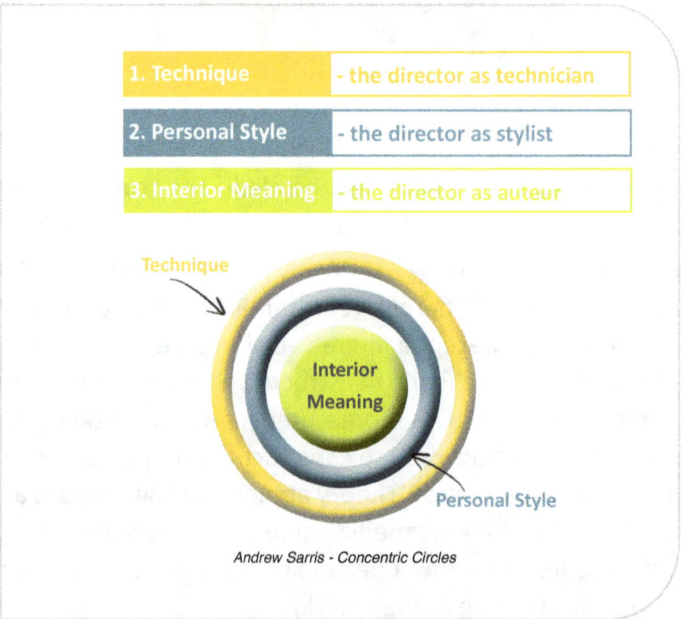

Andrew Sarris - Concentric Circles

1. Technique	- the director as technician
2. Personal Style	- the director as stylist
3. Interior Meaning	- the director as auteur

Summary of auteur theory

1963

Pauline Kael: Andrew Sarris' work caused significant debate and divide within the film world. His greatest known rival was Pauline Kael who responded with her 1963 essay *Circles and Squares* where she critically questioned the auteur theory by arguing that:

1. Kael suggests that **technical competence**, for the most part, is based on the judgement of the audience and critic, but she points out that in order to stretch boundaries, to be creative and experimental it is important to step aside from the standard template of what already exists and not allow a narrow definition of technical competence to limit the playbook of artistic expression.
2. Why should a director be congratulated for having a **distinctive style**, particularly when that style is simply different. She argued that directors do have varying styles seen across a body of work, this doesn't necessarily mark them as a good director. In fact, she proposes that the repetition of these stylistic elements by the director can become formulaic. She claims that the director has learnt how to manipulate the audience and simply delves into the same basket of tricks to repeat the performance in his or her next film.
3. Kael questions why substance in films is ignored and stylistic consistency praised.

AUTEUR THEORY PROS

- Acknowledges the consistent, distinctive, personal style of the filmmaker.

- Recognises the significant contribution of the director, often working within the confines of an institution.

- Identifies repetition in use of motifs and themes across a body of work.

- Recognises the filmmaker's personal vision and interior meaning.

- Recognises control over craft, specifically a heightened technical competence to show an innovative approach.

- The director is credited with having the principal creative vision; although overseeing many creative contributors, he/she is recognised for synthesising all ideas and output into a cohesive, stylistically consistent whole.

- A known director is easier to market as the audience can identify the style or innovative approach attributed to the director. Consider Wes Anderson, Tim Burton, and the Coen Brothers — how do marketers tap into the audiences' expectations of the style, technique, and personal vision of the director? Auteur branding, particularly trading on the name of the director, cultivates a fan base and creates recognition which assists with marketing.

AUTEUR THEORY CONS

- Film is built on a foundation of teamwork; it is a collaborative process. By looking at the end credits of any film you will be able to see the investment made by numerous skilled artists and technicians. Consider the Academy Awards given for artistic and technical contributions in film; these include Best Director, Best Actor in a Leading Role, Best Costume Designer, Best Cinematography, Best Film Editing, Best Original Score, Best Visual Effects, Best Original Screenplay and so on. John Williams has been nominated 51 times for his musical compositions for films such as Star Wars, Jaws, Jurassic Park, and the Harry Potter films to name a few. His significant contribution to these films would be largely ignored under the original design of the auteur theory. To ignore the contribution of all film personnel and only credit the director is antithetical to the film making process.

- Too much emphasis is placed on the director's singular vision in order to determine the worth of a film.

- Attributes worth to a director based on previous films rather than looking at each film in isolation.

Summary of genre theory

Genre theory - Stephen Neale: Repetition and difference
The audience has an expectation of the plot structure and events depending on the genre. Stephen Neale's theory of repetition and difference posits that the audience requires repetition for familiarity, however difference is required to maintain continued interest in the genre.

Stephen Neale, an Emeritus Professor of Film Studies at the University of Exeter posited in his 1980 book *Genre,* a theory of **repetition and difference** in which he states that genre elements provide pleasure to the audience as they are **identifiable** and contain **familiarity.** The familiarity provides comfort as the audience has distinguishable markers with which to navigate the narrative. However, Neale suggests that as comforting as identification of repeated elements are, the audience requires difference to be injected into the narrative to maintain continued interest in the genre (Neale, 1980, 48).

By departing from genre conventions, the audience and filmmaker enter an understanding regarding the incorporation of expected **genre conventions,** but find pleasure in the boundaries being shifted, with **difference** being incorporated into the plot.

Genre conventions act as a starting point or baseline which are understood by both the audience and filmmaker to create and negotiate narrative possibilities. It means that the audience understands what could happen based on their **familiarity** with previous films in the canon but enjoy the challenge of the filmmaker injecting **difference** to maintain audience engagement.

Neale's work lays the foundation for understanding how genres employ both **repetition and difference** to engage the audience by injecting unpredictability. The need for novelty or a twist of some sort has seen **sub-genres** and **genre hybridity** grow rapidly as it blends the familiar with the new.

GENRE CONVENTIONS

Genre conventions situate the audience to categorise films according to recognisable features and characteristics such as:
- Setting
- Character
- Motifs, symbols, iconography
- Narrative structure
- Style, codes, techniques
- Mood, tone

➡ Genres signal an understanding between audience and filmmaker.
➡ Genres become a frame of reference for decoding the narrative.
➡ Genres create a baseline which mediates how the viewer interprets the narrative.

Genres are not static, they evolve to reflect their cultural context.

Summary of identity theory

David Gauntlett, a British media theorist and sociologist specialises in the relationship between digital media and audiences. Gauntlett discusses the symbiotic relationship between consuming and creating in a digital landscape. He expresses how modern audiences, in their ability to produce their own media content, influence the construction of how their identity is represented.

Gauntlett argues that "identities are not 'given' but are constructed and negotiated" (Gauntlett, D. (2011). An audience draws a sense of their own identity from the media they consume, be it gender identity, sexual identity, or cultural identity. What does an audience learn about themselves from their media consumption and production?

Gauntlett contributes to the analysis of representations by providing the idea that media texts and social media platforms allow a modern audience to shape their own identities. Whereas historically media engagement was limited, and singular in the availability of representations of sexual orientation, race, body image, culture, and age; whereas nowadays a diversity of representations can be found due to the ease of access of independent media content found on the internet, which in turn influences mainstream practices. Therefore, people who previously struggled to find characters or stars to identify with now have a wider range of representations available to them.

The effect of social media culture on the construction and representation of gender cannot be under-estimated. Deconstructing how individuals make considered decisions when negotiating their on-line representation will reveal dominant ideologies about race, sexuality, and culture. In turn, these on-line representations surface in mainstream media, challenging dominant values and ideologies and questioning society's views on issues such as gender and sexuality.

Chapter Nine

Practice, organise, de-stress

- Notes pages
- Terminology practice
- Recommended viewing
- Recommended podcasts
- Recommended websites
- Recommended books
- De-stress colour-in pages
- QR codes for recommended Ted Talks

Practice, de-stress, recommendations

 Organise your thoughts

The final section of your journal contains space for you to write notes, record the websites, podcasts, books, and films that friends recommend in an organised manner, de-stress with some therapeutic colouring-in and watch some inspiring Ted Talks.

> MOTIVATION is what gets you started. HABIT is what keeps you going.
>
> Jim Ryun

 # Notes, notes, notes

Practice

Essential Content Notes

Essential Content Notes

Essential Content Notes

Essential Content Notes

Essential Content Notes

Essential Content Notes

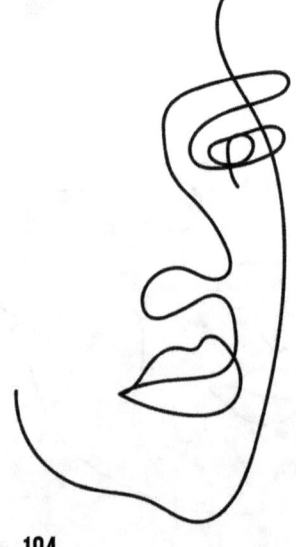

Essential Content Notes

Essential Content Notes

Essential Content Notes

Essential Content Notes

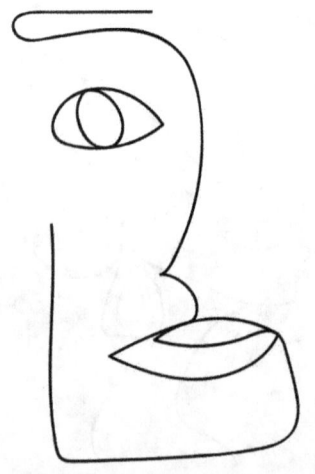

Essential Content Notes

Essential Content Notes

Essential Content Notes

Essential Content Notes

Essential Content Notes

Essential Content Notes

Essential Content Notes

Essential Content Notes

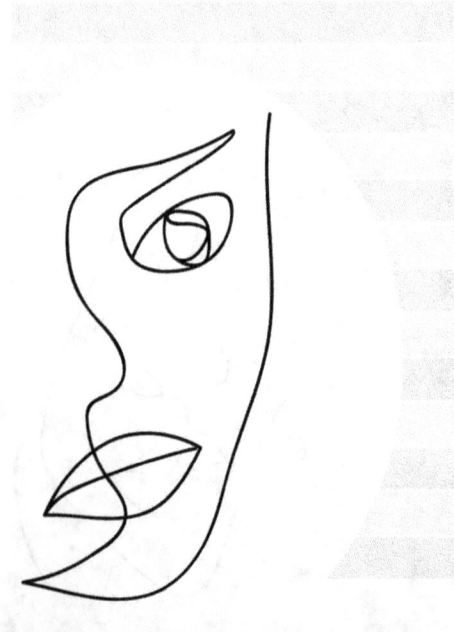

Essential Content Notes

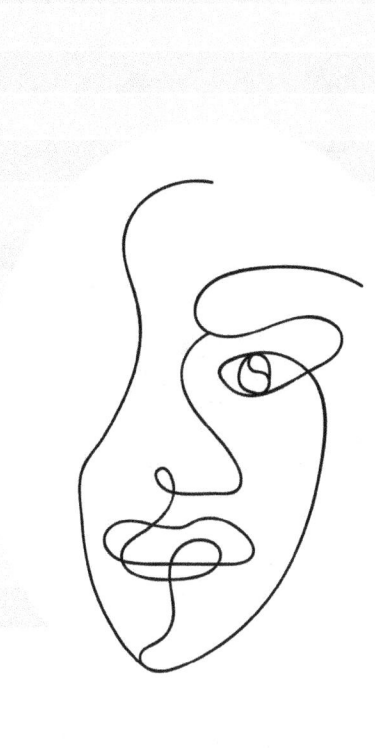

Essential Content Notes

Essential Content Notes

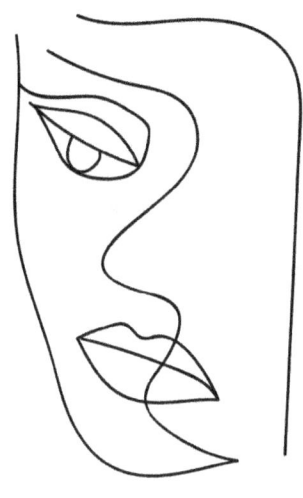

Essential Content Notes

Essential Content Notes

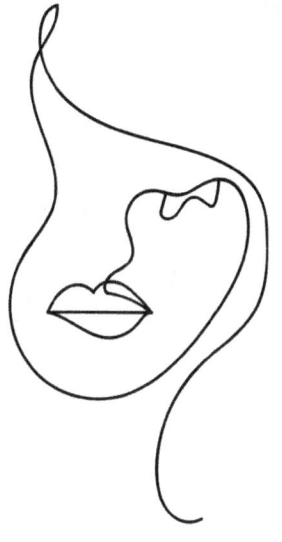

Essential Content Notes

Essential Content Notes

Essential Content Notes

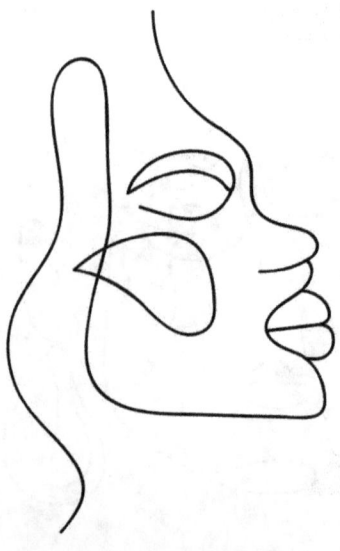

Essential Content Notes

Essential Content Notes

Essential Content Notes

Essential Content Notes

Essential Content Notes

Essential Content Notes

Essential Content Notes

Essential Content Notes

Essential Content Notes

Essential Content Notes

Essential Content Notes

Essential Content Notes

Essential Content Notes

Essential Content Notes

Essential Content Notes

Essential Content Notes

Essential Content Notes

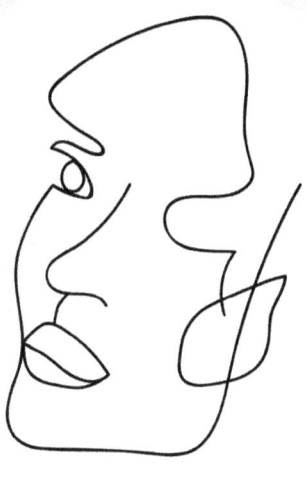

Essential Content Notes

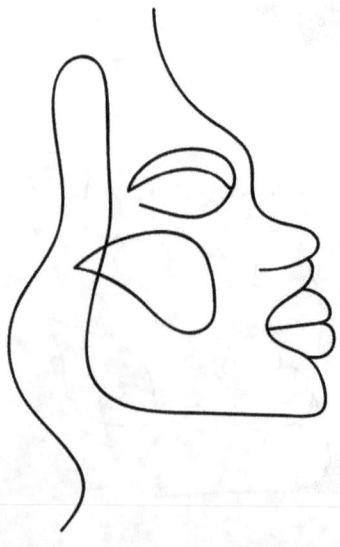

Essential Content Notes

Essential Content Notes

Essential Content Notes

Media Terminology

AUTEUR

AUTEUR THEORY

POPULAR CULTURE

CODES

Media TERMINOLOGY

CONVENTIONS

MAINSTREAM AUDIENCE

NICHE AUDIENCE

SUBCULTURE

Media TERMINOLOGY

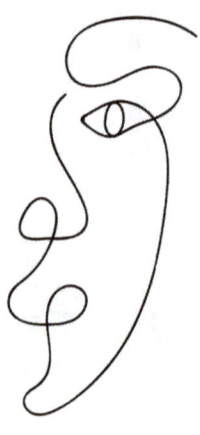

CONTEXT

NARRATIVE ELEMENTS

TODOROV'S THEORY

BINARY OPPOSITIONS

Media TERMINOLOGY

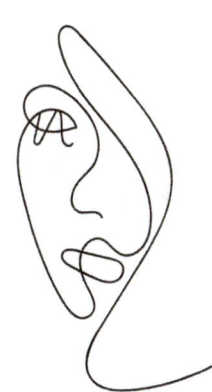

POINT OF VIEW

NARRATIVE MANIPULATION

NARRATIVE STRUCTURE

ENCODING, DECODING

Media TERMINOLOGY

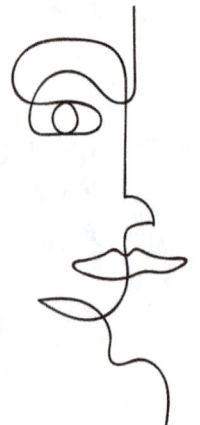

REALISM

CONTROLS AND CONSTRAINTS

MEDIA OWNERSHIP ISSUES

CENSORSHIP

Media TERMINOLOGY

CLASSIFICATION

COMMERCIAL MEDIA

INDEPENDENT MEDIA

ALTERNATE MEDIA

Media TERMINOLOGY

PERSONAL EXPRESSION

CONNOTATION

DENOTATION

PRIMARY AUDIENCE

Media TERMINOLOGY

SECONDARY AUDIENCE

AUDIENCE REACH

MANIPULATION OF TIME

MANIPULATION OF SPACE

Media TERMINOLOGY

CINEMA VERITE

REPRESENTATION

STEREOTYPE

REPRESENTATION STUART HALL

Media TERMINOLOGY

PROBLEMS WITH STEREOTYPING

ATTITUDES, BELIEFS

VALUES

IDEOLOGIES

Media TERMINOLOGY

COMMUNICATION THEORIES

RECEPTION THEORY

REINFORCEMENT THEORY

USES & GRATIFICATIONS THEORY

Media TERMINOLOGY

AGENDA SETTING THEORY

CULTIVATION THEORY

SPIRAL OF SILENCE

DIFFUSION OF INNOVATION

Media TERMINOLOGY

DOCUMENTARY CONVENTIONS

DOCUMENTARY TECHNIQUES

PRODUCTION CONTEXT

RECEPTION CONTEXT

Media TERMINOLOGY

GLOBALISATION

CONGLOMERATES

PERSUASIVE TECHNIQUES

PROPAGANDA

Media TERMINOLOGY

MEDIA TRENDS

TECHNOLOGICAL TRENDS

SOCIAL TRENDS

SELECTION, OMISSION

Media TERMINOLOGY

IMMEDIACY

ACCESSIBILITY

ETHICAL & LEGAL ISSUES

INFLUENTIAL MEDIA

Media TERMINOLOGY

PREFERRED MEANING

OPPOSITIONAL MEANING

NEGOTIATED MEANING

THEME

Media TERMINOLOGY

FILM MOVEMENTS

FILM NOIR

GERMAN EXPRESIONISM

SURREALISM

Media TERMINOLOGY

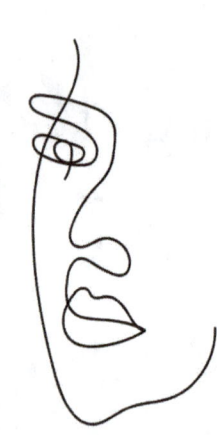

FRENCH NEW WAVE

PRODUCTION, DISTRIBUTION

EXHIBITION, MARKETING

FUNDING

Media TERMINOLOGY

DIEGETIC

NON-DIEGETIC

GENRE

ICONOGRAPHY

Media TERMINOLOGY

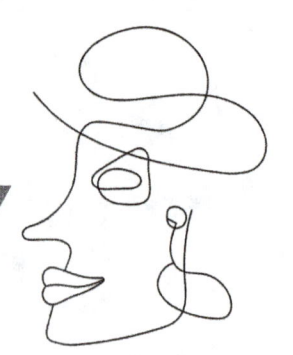

VISUAL MOTIF

AURAL MOTIF

MISE-EN-SCENE

THEME

Media TERMINOLOGY

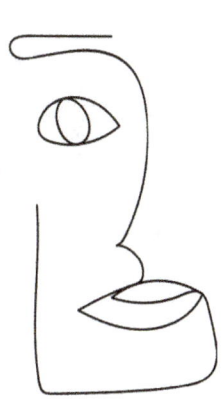

GENRE THEORY STEPHEN NEALE

GLOBAL ACCESS

SOCIAL OR POLITICAL COMMENT

SELECTION PROCESSES

Media TERMINOLOGY

ANTAGONIST

PROTAGONIST

CHARACTER ARC

EDITORIAL CONTROL

Media TERMINOLOGY

TEMPORAL ORDER

TEMPORAL FREQUENCY

TEMPORAL DURATION

HEGEMONY

Media TERMINOLOGY

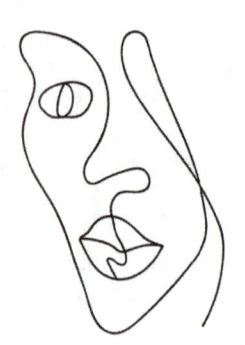

DISCOURSE

COUNTER DISCOURSE

CULTURAL CONTEXT

AUDIENCE DEMOGRAPHICS

Media TERMINOLOGY

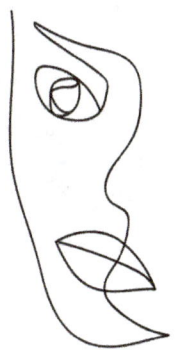

MONTAGE

FREYTAG'S PYRAMID

MEDIA THEORY

EXPOSITION

Media TERMINOLOGY

Media TERMINOLOGY

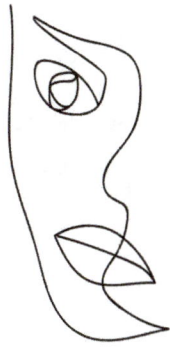

Media TERMINOLOGY

Media TERMINOLOGY

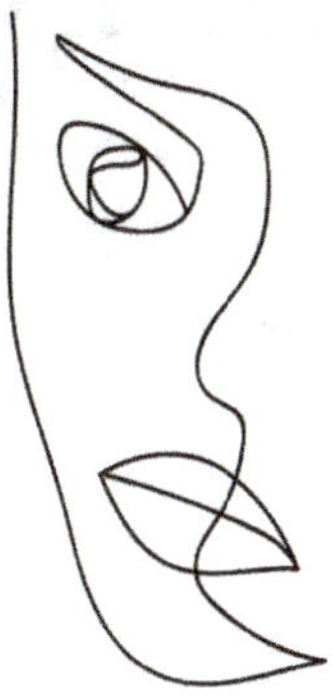

Film & TV recommendations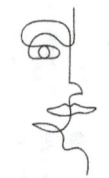

Recommended Viewing

 **Podcast recommendations**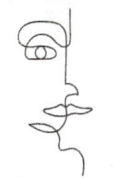

Recommended Listening

Website recommendations

Recommended Websites

Book recommendations

Recommended Reading

Colour-in
Relax

REFOCUS YOUR BRAIN

Not just for children, there is scientific evidence regarding the benefits of colouring-in. The repetitive nature of colouring a complex design like a mandala relaxes the brain and aids in stress management. Take a brain break and colour-in one of the mandalas to relax and refocus when you need a study break.

Colour-in, de-stress, relax

Colour-in
Relax

Colour-in
De-stress

Interesting Ted talks

Ted Talks & Others

01	Danger of a single story. Chimamanda Adichie.
02	Inside the mind of a master procrastinator. Tim Urban.
03	The shared experience of absurdity. Charlie Todd.
04	Your body language may shape who you are. Amy Cuddy.
05	Don't eat the marshmallow! Joachim de Posada.
06	The unheard story of David and Goliath. Malcolm Gladwell.
07	The windows and mirrors of your child's bookshelf. Grace Lin.
08	The danger of silence. Clint Smith.
09	Connected, but alone? Sherry Turkle.
10	We need to talk about an injustice. Bryan Stevenson.
11	Do schools kill creativity? Sir Ken Robinson.
12	Living beyond limits. Amy Purdy.
13	Why some of us don't have one true calling. Emilie Wapnick
14	Grit: The power of passion and perseverance. Angela Lee Duckworth.
15	How to stay calm when you know you'll be stressed. Daniel Levitin.
16	What your grades really mean. Eva Ren.
17	The power of vulnerability. Brené Brown.
18	Looks aren't everything. Believe me, I'm a model. Cameron Russell.

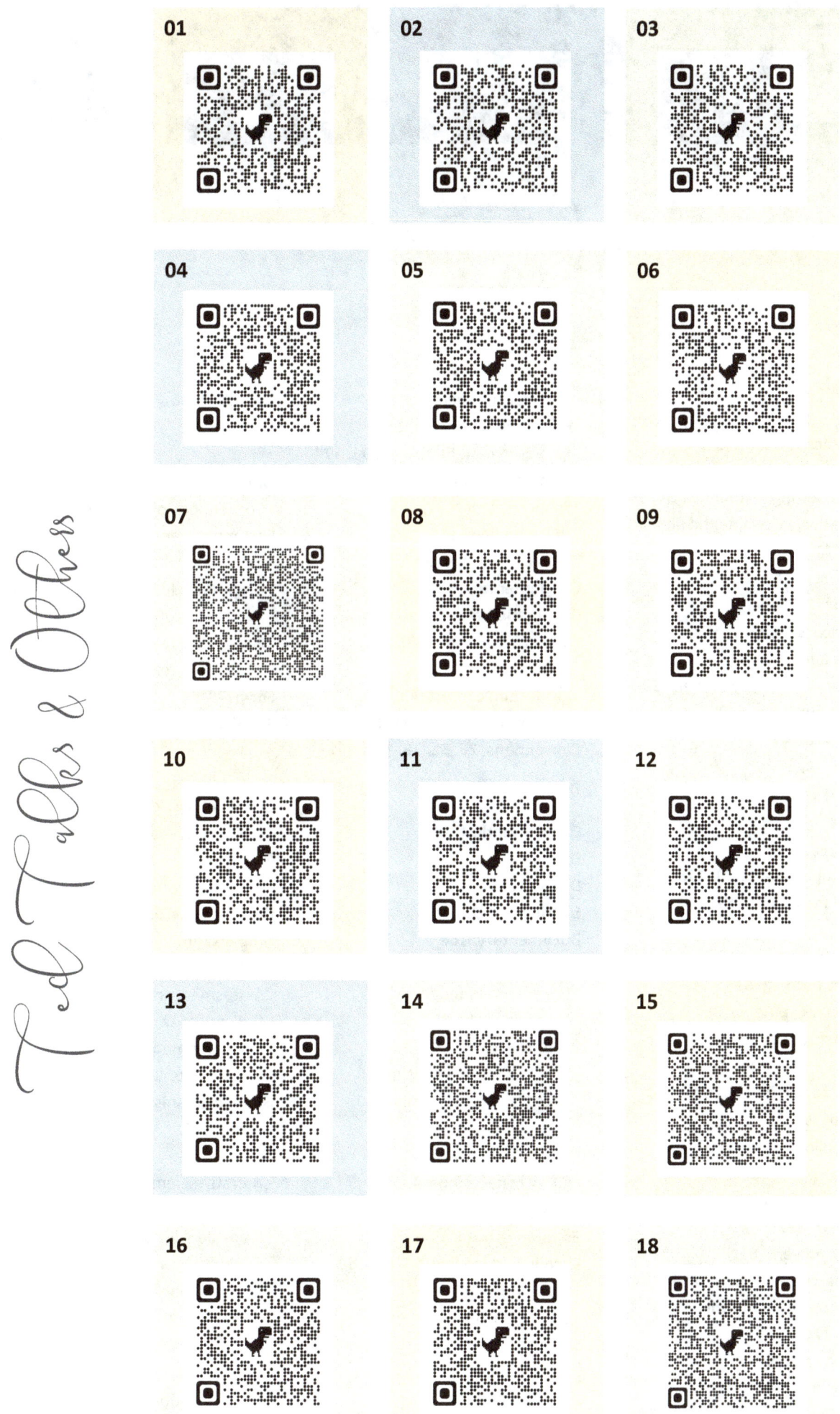

Index

Where to find bits & bobs

A

Aesthetics 44, 62, 165
Agenda 57
Agenda setting techniques 54, 66
Alternative, experimental film 46, 70
Artistic style 46
Attitudes 35
Audience 35, 62, 77, 153, 163
  Niche audience 49, 63
  Primary, secondary, tertiary 35
  Target audience 140
Aural motif 47
Auteur 44, 67
  Auteur Theory 167, 182

B

Binary oppositions 71, 178
Bloom's taxonomy 81

C

Camera framing 87
Camera movements 86
Censorship 51, 54
Cinema verite 50
Codes 19, 32, 76, 140, 150, 161
  Audio 19, 22, 33, 67, 75
  Symbolic 19, 20, 32, 62, 75
  Technical 19, 23, 24, 25, 33, 64, 75
  Written 19, 21, 33, 66, 75
Colour-in 272
Command verb 81, 82
Commercial, non-commercial 57
Communication theories 35, 152, 174
  Agenda setting theory 36, 175
  Cultivation theory 37, 175
  Diffusion of innovation 37, 175
  Hypodermic needle 36, 174
  Reception theory 36, 175
  Reinforcement theory 37, 71, 174
  Semiotic theory 174
  Spiral of silence 37, 175
  Two step flow 174
  Uses and Gratifications 36, 71, 175
Conglomerates 57
Connotation and denotation 33
Context 40, 65, 76, 140, 151, 164
  Cultural context 55
  Production context 43, 56, 167
Controls and constraints 42, 156
Conventions 26, 32, 78, 150, 161

D

David Gauntlett 185
Diegesis 51
Discourse 41
Distribution 58
Documentary 168
  Conventions 56
  Documentary modes 52
  Techniques 42, 67
Drop-down list 149
  Year 11 drop-down lists 150
  Year 12 drop-down lists 160

E

Editing conventions 47
Editing techniques 70, 78, 89
Editorial control 53
Encoding, decoding 56, 64, 180
Essay structure 93
  Essay plan 95
  Structure strips 104
  T.E.E.L model 94
  T.E.E.L structure example 99
Exhibition 58

F

Film art 45
  Conventions of art films 45
Film movements 45
Flashcards
  Drop-down list Year 11 & 12 flash cards 60
  Flash cards Year 11 32
  Flash cards Year 12 44
Form 78
Funding 52, 70

G

Genre 40, 66, 79
  Genre conventions 184
Genre theory - Stephen Neale 184
  Genre Conventions 184
Global access 55
Globalisation 53, 157
Goal setting 9
  Assessment tracker 14
  Due dates 12
  Revision timetable 13
  Study habits 10
Graphic organiser 107
  Codes 142
  Context 145
  Narrative elements 144
  Representations 147
  Study booklet 110
  Study flash card 108
  Target audience 143
  Values and ideologies 146

H

Hall's Reception Theory 63

Index

Hegemony 51

I

Iconic figure 45
Identity theory
  David Gauntlett 185
Identity Theory 185
Ideology 34, 64, 77, 153, 164, 171
Independent film 46, 63, 166
Industry issues 54
Institutions 53, 80, 157, 166

M

Mainstream culture 34
Mainstream film 69
Manipulation of space 50, 69
Manipulation of time 50, 69
Marketing 56
Media influence 42, 159
Media ownership 42
Media Terminology 237
Media theories 55, 62, 154, 173
Mise-en-scene 43
Montage 40, 65
Motif
  Aural motif 47
  Visual motif 47

N

Narrative 61, 74, 154, 162
Narrative conventions 49, 170
Narrative elements 38, 140
Narrative manipulation 49
Narrative structure 38, 48
Narrative theories 39
  Binary oppositions 39, 71, 178
  Claude Levi-Strauss 178
  Freytag 39, 176
  Joseph Campbell 48, 178
  Roland Barthes 48, 179
  Syd Field 48, 177
  Todorov 38, 71, 176
  Vladimir Propp 49, 177
Niche audience 49, 63
Notes Pages 189

P

Personal expression 46, 69
Persuasive techniques 53, 65, 156
Point of view 38, 61, 155
Popular culture 34, 80
Preferred meaning 158
Production context 167
Propaganda 51, 68, 168
Publicity 58

Q

Quoting 101
  Direct quotes 102
  In-text citation 103

R

Realism 43
Reception theory 63
Recommended Listening 267
Recommended Reading 269
Recommended Viewing 266
Recommended Websites 268
Regulations 54
Reinforcement theory 71
Representation 41, 61, 76, 141, 151, 162
  Gauntlett 52
Representation Theory 180
  Stuart Hall 55, 180, 181
Revision 16

S

Selection, omission 52, 66, 158
Selection processes 57
Sentence starters & stems 84
Setting 67
Shared cultural maps 180, 181
Signal verb 100
Social, political comment 54, 68
Sound 88
Stereotypes 41, 141
  Naturalisation of stereotypes 50, 68
  Problems with stereotyping 44, 68
Subculture 41, 61, 152, 163

T

Ted Talks 274
Television 78
Television narrative 39
Theme 40, 63, 79, 159
Todorov's theory 71
Transition words 85
Trends 43, 47, 65, 80, 155, 165

U

Uses and gratifications 71

V

Values 34, 64, 77, 141, 153, 164, 171
Visual motif 47

Bibliography

Borowitz, A., & Borowitz, S. (Writers) & Allen, D. (Director).(1990). The Fresh Prince Project (Season 1 Episode 1) In Jones, Q (Executive Producer), *The Fresh Prince of Bel Air.* NBC.

ChallengingMedia (2006, October 4) *Representation and the Media: Featuring Stuart Hall.* [Video] Youtube. https://www.youtube.com/watch?v=aTzMsPqssOY

Clear, J. (2018) Atomic Habits: An Easy & Proven Way to Build Good Habits & Break Bad Ones. Penguin Publishing Group.

Gambino, C. [Donald Glover].(2018). *This is America. Official Video* [Video] Youtube. https://www.youtube.com/watch?v=VYOjWnS4cMY

Gauntlett, D. (2018). Making is connecting: The social power of creativity, from craft and knitting to digital everything. John Wiley & Sons.

Gillette. (2019). We Believe: *The Best Men Can Be* | Gillette (Advertisement) [YouTube Video]. https://www.youtube.com/watch?v=koPmuEyP3a0

Hall, S (1997). *Representation: cultural representation and signifying practices.* The Open University.

Kael, P. (1963). Circles and squares. Film Quarterly, 16(3), 12-26.

Merante, L. (2022). Media Analysis: Understanding and Applying Media Theory in Year 11. Media and English Literacy Publishing.

Neale, S. (1980). *Genre.* (Edition 3) British Film Institute.

Truffaut, F. (1954). Une certaine tendance du cinéma français. Cahiers du cinéma, 31(31).

Wilson, L. O. (2016). Anderson and Krathwohl–Bloom's taxonomy revised. Understanding the New Version of Bloom's Taxonomy.

The following **four books** work in conjunction with one another to assist in building a strong knowledge base to equip students with the necessary skills to confidently succeed in Media Production and Analysis.

1. Media Analysis: Understanding and Applying Media Theory - Year 11
2. Media Analysis: Understanding and Applying Media Theory - Year 12 (available late 2023)
3. Media Analysis Compendium - Year 11 and 12
4. Media Production Journal - Year 11 and 12

www.ingramcontent.com/pod-product-compliance
Lightning Source LLC
Chambersburg PA
CBHW080856010526
44107CB00058B/2600